THE SILENT WITN

Peter Brent and David Rolfe

The Silent Witness

Futura Publications Limited
A Futura Book

A Futura Book

First published in Great Britain by
Futura Publications Limited in 1978

TO JACQ'
Without whose patience, help and encouragement *The Silent Witness* would never have been made.

ISBN 0 7088 1438 7

Printed by
William Collins Sons & Co Ltd
Glasgow

Futura Publications Limited,
110 Warner Road, Camberwell,
London SE5.

Contributors

Dr Robert Bucklin	Forensic Pathologist
Captain John P. Jackson, USAF	Physicist and Assistant Professor, Air Force Academy
Dr Eric Jumper, Captain, USAF	Assistant Professor of Aerodynamics, Air Force Academy
Dr Donald Lynn	Supervisor, Image Enhancement, Jet Propulsion Laboratory
Monsignor Giulio Ricci	Author of *La Sindone Santa* published by Centro Romano di Sindonologia, Via Borga Angelico 14, Rome
Rt Rev Dr John A. T. Robinson	Dean of Trinity College, Cambridge – Lecturer in Theology
Dr Max Frei Sulzer	Criminologist and Botanist
Ian Wilson, MA (Oxon)	Historian. Author of *The Turin Shroud*

The Silent Witness: Film Credits

Written by IAN WILSON, HENRY LINCOLN, DAVID W. ROLFE
Produced and directed by DAVID W. ROLFE

Executive Producers
Adam J. Otterbein CSSR, STD
Peter M. Rinaldi SDB, MA

Photography: Bahram Manocheri
Editor: Peter Hollywood

Assistant to the Producer: Sandra Fox
Production Manager: Roger Connolly
Sound Recordist: Wally Plummer
Art Director: Tony Halton
Assistant Editor: Edward Marnier
Costume Supervisor: Ivy Baker-Jones
Assistant Director: Leszek Burzynski
Chief Gaffer: Larry Prinz
Assistant Sound Recordist: John Chandler
Assistant Sound Recordist: David Gatrell
Production Secretary: Linda Taylor
Dubbing Editor: Edward Mason
Dubbing Mixer: Tony Anscombe
Picture Researcher: Mary Rose-Richards
Continuity: Marion Allinson
Make-up Supervisor: Penny Delamar
Property Buyer: Bill Sawyer
Prop. Man: Jack West
General Assistant: Brian Deliglas

Turkish Location:
Co-ordinator: Samim Deger

French Location:
Co-ordinator: Patricia Warren

Italian Location:
Co-ordinator: Manrico Melchiore

Icon Painting by St Seraphim's Brotherhood
Film processed by Humphries Film Laboratories
Set construction by Cinebuild

ARTISTES

Secondo Pia played by Richard Hamer

Other characters played by:	Sarah Twist
	Angela Ellis
	Daphne Odin-Pearse
	Barry Cranfield
	David Harris
	Ramon St Clair
	Andy Kontouri
Music Advisor	Ted Davis
Special Music composed by	Alan Hawkshaw
Special Construction and Design	John Weston
Assistant Cameraman	Paul Turtle
Clapper Loader	Jamie Harcourt

The Producers would like to thank the following for their help in the making of *The Silent Witness*:

DE RANCE FOUNDATION
HOLY SHROUD GUILD OF AMERICA
INTERNATIONAL CENTRE OF SINDONOLOGY, TURIN
BRITISH SOCIETY FOR THE TURIN SHROUD
UNITED STATES AIR FORCE ACADEMY, COLORADO
OFFICE OF THE MEDICAL EXAMINER AND CORONER, LOS ANGELES COUNTY
TRINITY COLLEGE, CAMBRIDGE
ST JOHN'S COLLEGE, CAMBRIDGE
MAGDELEN COLLEGE, OXFORD
THE PARISH OF TEMPLECOMBE
THE MAYOR AND PEOPLE OF LIREY, FRANCE
THE MAYOR AND PEOPLE OF CHAMBERY, FRANCE
THE METROPOLITAN AND PAROCHIAL AUTHORITIES OF ST JOHN'S CATHEDRAL, TURIN
DON PIERO COERO BORGA
'THE HOLY SUDARIUM' REPRODUCED BY GRACIOUS PERMISSION OF HER MAJESTY THE QUEEN
MUSEO NAZIONALE DEL CINEMA, TURIN, ITALY

My thanks are due to so many people for making both the film *The Silent Witness* and this book possible that it would take an entire chapter just to list them. I only hope that these few words can echo my sincere gratitude to them all.

I would like to take this opportunity, however, to put on record my admiration for and gratitude to Naim Attallah who, alone amongst those who saw the film when it was first completed, had the foresight, determination and indeed courage, to give the film an opportunity for a public release. Those who have seen and enjoyed the film owe their experience largely to his faith in the project.

In a similar vein, the help, advice and patience I received from Rodney Collins of Barclays Bank, Wardour Street was invaluable and contributed greatly to the success of the film.

I should like to pay a special tribute to my assistant Sandra Fox who followed the varying fortunes of the project from the beginning with unswerving loyalty, dedication and, equally importantly, a sense of humour and friendliness which brought and held together, even during the rough patches, all who contributed to the film.

Lastly, not so much of a thank you but congratulations to Peter Brent who, I think, has done a splendid job of recounting in such an interesting way the narration and background to this extraordinary project. I am sure you will enjoy it.

D.W.R.
London, 22nd May 1978.

INTRODUCTION

The priests stand clustered on the high platform. Their vestments shine in the pale North European sun. Music plays; at the foot of the platform a choir sings, the sweet voices rising in anthems toward the tree tops. A deep baritone of a prayer, an invocation, follows. Beyond the bright circle of ritual, staring in expectation upward at the platform, a silent crowd stands pressed together. The bright robes of the rich, the dun jerkins of the poor; perhaps a tent or two, a brilliant pennant; perhaps a tall pavilion guarding the slim ladies of the nobility, the chattering ladies with their elaborate headdresses and their jewelled girdles. Seated above their kerchiefed peasant sisters, they feel nevertheless bound with them, with every person there, in an unbearable and totally absorbing curiosity.

And then the moment that has gathered them – the monks stepping solemnly forward, the long cloth slowly unfolded, opened like some book to be read, finally hoisted high in the restless summer air and extended towards the waiting people. There is a great collective sigh from the crowd, a long moan of reverence and wonder. 'The Shroud!' people are saying, more to themselves than to each other. 'The Shroud! Look, look – it's the Shroud of Christ!'

And there indeed, glimpsed from a distance, shimmering in the sunlight, an image hangs before them, *the* image, the ultimate manifestation, the final evidence of the central power of their faith. And, it may be that, at this moment, the trumpets yell in triumph and the high voices of the choristers rise and rise in frenzied exultation

We may assume such a scene, imagine or recreate the moment when, in the village of Lirey, the piece of linen claimed to be the Shroud of Jesus was first shown to a European audience. There, amid the bright greenery of France, and to the disturbance of at least some of the ecclesiastical authorities, it was placed regularly on exhibition during the middle years of the fourteenth century. The display of relics was common enough in those days, and this one was not essentially different from any of the others. We remember it only because of the mysterious nature of the object displayed, the hauntingly inexplicable genesis of the image it bears and the centuries of speculation and, more recently, of research which have left us apparently still on the brink of miracle. Does the Shroud show the genuine imprint of the face and body of Christ? If it does not, whose does it show? And, whoever it displays, how was that imprint made?

In our century historians have, in a sense, had to give way to scientists in the effort to authenticate or discredit this strange relic. Strangely, it is the historians who have largely doubted its genuineness, while it is the scientists, despite the agnostics and even atheists among them, who have come to its defence. To be sure, their findings have on the whole been negative contributions – the Shroud can only be proved not to have been faked. The fact is, however, that no method of forging it thus far proposed has passed scientific scrutiny. The areas of possibility narrows – and continues to include the miraculous.

Over the centuries, naturally enough, the Shroud has at intervals continued to be put on exhibition. It has had several resting places, several centres at which such displays were held. It is now, as it has been since 1578, in Turin Cathedral. Today, however, we have devised new methods for the exposition of objects that interest us. We have television and we have film. We do not need to travel in our pilgrim thousands to Turin, on those rare occasions – two or three times in a hundred years – when the Shroud is brought out for the public to gaze at it. We can, as it were, sit back and have it brought to us. Nor, when it is so brought, do we have to be content with a distant view, snatched from behind a pillar or over the shoulders of the reverent. We can see it, clearly, in detail, filling the screen in front of us.

This book is about all these matters. It is about the Holy Shroud of Turin. It is about the arguments, both historical and scientific, concerning its authenticity. It is about the research over the last decade to resolve those arguments. It details precisely where that scientific effort is today. And the book is about the making of a film, *The Silent Witness*, which is the clearest and most penetrating attempt yet made to place the Shroud before us without cant or preconception, without the bias of either piety or scepticism. It is, necessarily, also about the people who made the film and what their feelings were, for the Shroud and, unavoidably, for each other.

Because it is partly the work of David Rolfe, the man who also made the film, this book can claim to be factually correct: not only in its approach to that production, but also in what it says about the research, much of which Rolfe himself co-ordinated, and about the historical theories upon which the film was based. But the book is only partly David's work. The involvement of another writer, Peter Brent, who was not at all concerned in the making of the film nor in Shroud investigations, permit it an objectivity it might otherwise have lacked. Thus it can look at the Shroud and its implications from a standpoint other than that of the film. It can look at the film itself with the eye of an outsider. It is an independent entity, not a 'book of the film'. For that reason it uses the third person pronoun for David Rolfe, despite his presence on the cover as co-author.

Its central subject, however, remains the Holy Shroud of Turin. At the least, the Shroud is an object of absorbing interest, an artifact created by processes that defy the most refined analyses of contemporary technology. At the most, it is physical evidence for the life and agonising death of a

Person who may have been God, a record of one of the most significant moments – perhaps the most significant – in the history of the world. If it is what it seems, then more powerfully than anything else on earth it is what David Rolfe has called it – The Silent Witness.

CHAPTER ONE

The face, a nebulous white and grey against the black background, shimmered across the surface of the photograph. Long hair fell about its features. In the nose, the long, slightly pouched cheeks, the wide, downturned mouth and the broad, fork-bearded chin, there were indications of great strength. The eyes were closed. The expression was one of determined resignation, the acceptance of some abominable fate. Two white lines cut like lightning streaks across the picture, and incomprehensible stains marked the forehead. As David Rolfe leaned closer, he saw that the whole face was printed in a peculiar herringbone pattern, as though upon a cloth. For a moment longer, he stared, fascinated, at this strange photograph, then turned to the flimsily-bound manuscript from which it had fallen.

The first question – whose face was it? – was answered by the title: *He Is Risen .. The story of the Holy Shroud of Christ*. He had been looking at what purported to be the face of Jesus. He was very tired, but so extraordinary a claim produced a resonance of excitement and curiosity. What was this Holy Shroud? Rolfe had never heard of it. Was it fact or fiction? Was he looking at a drama, an investigation or a hoax? And the man who had written the manuscript, Ian Wilson, who was he and what were his qualifications? Settling back into the comfort of his couch, surrounded by the bright walls and efficient paraphernalia of his modern office high above Wardour Street, he prepared himself to read about marvels ...

David Rolfe was the product of the complex, rather coarse-grained educational processes of a comprehensive school. He was twelve when he had declared, to the outraged laughter of his teacher, his ambition to become a television producer. In a socially stratified Britain, everyone is supposed to know very early in life the limits of what they can hope for. Films and television, in something more than a tea-boy capacity, were not intended for the likes of young David. He thought otherwise. Sixth Form college brought him a pair of A-level passes. He might have gone to university. Instead, he went straight to where he thought the heart of what he wanted lay – to the BBC in London.

For a while, it hardly mattered that his was among the lowest and dustiest rungs in that bureaucracy's vast ladder. Every day he clipped out articles and items from newspapers chosen by some pencil-wielding senior. No chance for initiative, nor for intelligence more exacting than that needed to place the right piece of paper in the right drab file. Day by day, the brown boxes of miscellaneous information rose higher and settled more threateningly into wall and bastions. In this paper prison, hope and excitement shrivelled into disenchantment. Not only his work, the BBC itself, its self-absorption, its complacency, the feeling that being 'a BBC man' should be more than sufficient to sustain one, began to suffocate him. The canteen talk of BBC programmes and BBC politics and BBC personalities began to sound like an endless dirge.

Nevertheless, he progressed; he was now actually searching out the cuttings and clippings that hitherto he had only filed away. And two or three evenings a week, he would run messages for the presenters of the current affairs programmes. He was closer to the cameras, closer to the realities of how information was processed, closer therefore to his ambition. Yet disenchantment deepened. He could see now how vain where all protestations of 'objectivity' in a medium where there was never time enough to present the various relevant views in any depth, and where the supremacy of the presenters meant that, in the last analysis, their viewpoint prevailed. It seemed to him, too, that these facts reinforced the arrogance and claustrophobia he felt in that institution. It was time to seek fresher air.

After a period working as a freelance photographer – a little ironically, the BBC was among his best customers – he enrolled in the London International Film School. Now began a period of hectic effort and thin rewards. He felt at odds with the aims of the students around him. They wanted to be directors; nothing less was enough for them. To be producer of one of the small student movies was, therefore, an unpopular role. Thus, on the films on which David worked, it was he who, whatever his other responsibilities, would frequently take over the chores of the producer.

It is the producer who guides the whole project off the scriptwriter's page and into the studio, gathering together the team whose talents will shape it into colour, speech and drama, provide whatever is needed – a herd of zebras, a tightrope walker, an army corps. He also modifies and monitors the work being done by writers, directors, actors and editors. He is the presiding *dei* over a temporary cosmos, created by him for a single purpose – the making of a film. It is no despicable way to employ one's talents.

David was one of the fifteen per cent who graduated from the school with honours. His first 'real' film was a short documentary, *Environmental Engineering – A New Challenge*. There have, in the history of the cinema, been more inspiring assignments. However, you make what you can of what is offered you: this unpretentious film turned out to be, at its own level, a distinct success. Mildly euphoric, and in the hope of further commissions to come, David formed his own company.

For six months nothing at all happened. Eventually, however, the Films Officer of a construction company, constantly faced with the problem of trying to make fairly dull subjects lively, spotted David's talent in that direction. He offered him work on scripts, and other, similar concerns followed suit. Soon he was busily traversing the Iberian Peninsula and the oil states of the Middle East working on projects thrown up by those booming economies.

With a partner, he then spent eighteen profitable months making trailers, title sequences and all the other ancillary work that big feature films require. The British movie industry then began to decline. With fewer commissions arriving, his partner joined one of the more important film companies. In his office high above Wardour Street, looking out over the rooftops of the mighty stretching away to the north and his mornings made delicious by the smells floating up from bakery and the coffee grinders' below, David worked on alone.

Sponsored films were, however, now as difficult to set up as those for public viewing. An argument which could be turned on its head. One could say that films designed for public distribution were now no more difficult to fund than sponsored films. In partnership with a young American journalist, Susan Francis, he set up the Film and Television Script Company, through which he hoped to discover the only raw material apart from energy and talent that he needed, viable projects. The company received scripts and outlines, made short synopses of them, and circulated these to potential producers. David's own production company, therefore, had a constant source of new ideas which he was the first to see.

He began by contacting the press and by advertising. The world heard him. From every corner of the country, and beyond (the furthest afield being Livingstone, today's Zambian township of Maramba), in plastic folders and cardboard boxes, bound with ribbon, string or tape, stapled, sealed with sticking plaster or flopping confusingly from torn brown envelopes, the outpourings of the screen-struck arrived in an overwhelming wave. Hastily he stopped the advertising campaign. Peering dismally at the piled-up manuscripts, he began to realise that the cost in time needed to read so many had destroyed his scheme before it had properly begun. Nevertheless, both he and his partner felt an obligation to these regiments of the obscure and ambitious who had responded to their call. Grimly, they settled down to read their way through everything that had been sent them and to write both a short outline and a curt opinion for each single manuscript.

Unfortunately very little originality, talent or professionalism was apparent. At first optimism gave rise to kindly comments such as 'Zany humour', or 'Interesting combination of characters' or 'Well written'. But this expectant, positive mood soon passed; the comments took on a darker nature. 'Confusing ... Little originality ... Rather silly ... Not original', descending after a while to 'Boring, trite ... sub-standard' and 'Weak plot ... V dreary', to the simple 'Bad' and the even simpler 'NG'.

One can imagine, then, David's frame of mind when, on a late-autumn day in 1974, he picked up the last but one of the enormous pile of contributions. He might have been forgiven if he had done no more than skim through, almost sightlessly, the typewritten pages of these two final manuscripts. And so he might have done – if that photograph had not fallen to the floor and, bending down, he had not been confronted by the profound pain and mystery of that shimmering face.

In a mood of astonished and astonishing excitement, David read through the fifty foolscap pages of Ian Wilson's script. He took it home that evening and read it again. In the morning, on the train into town, he read it a third time. Again and again he turned to the pictures Wilson had thoughtfully provided: photographs of icons and paintings and of the Shroud itself. Again and again he stared at that long-jawed, bearded face, secret in its strength and anguish, as though determined to penetrate its mystery. The feeling that he had found something extraordinary, the exact ingredient he had been searching for, possessed him almost physically.

He was an agnostic, perhaps even an atheist. He had forbidden his parents to take his daughter to church. The one occasion when they had done so had led to a quarrel. He regarded the church as, in his own words, 'an area full of medieval numbo-jumbo'. He considered it illogical and pointless. He resented its very existence. His upbringing, nominally Christian, had been conventionally irreligious. But now he felt that if he, in this near-atheistic frame of mind, could be fascinated by a religious subject, so might other people, in which case some of those people might be persuaded to underwrite a film about it. He had, in this thesis about the origins of the Holy Shroud of Turin, the basis of a cinematic project for which he could hope to raise money. He had found what he was looking for.

Yet what was the Shroud? His knowledge extended no further than the script. It lay, apparently, in a silver-mounted casket within a great iron chest guarded by a solid metal grille, in the ornate interior of Turin cathedral. For centuries this fourteen-foot length of ancient linen had belonged to the House of Savoy, Italy's royal family. On that cloth, faintly visible, was the full-length image of a man. The image was double – one of the front of the man, the other of the back. The man had been placed on the cloth, his feet near one end, and the long other end had then been folded over his face and stretched down the front of his body to his feet again. In some way, the impression of this apparent corpse had then been created or left upon the linen. It showed that before death he had been much abused. There were marks on his head, at his wrists, in his side and at his ankles, that were clearly runnels of blood. The man had been crucified and then left this curious impress on the sheet that covered him and vanished – into obscurity or into world history?

Ian Wilson, the writer of the script, seemed to have few doubts. For him the cloth kept in Turin was the one described by St John: Mary Magdalene had seen that the stone had been rolled away from the entrance to Jesus's temporary tomb. 'Then she runneth and cometh to Simon Peter, and to the other disciple, whom Jesus loved, and said unto them, They have taken away the Lord out of the sepulchre ... So they ran both together and the other disciple did outrun Peter and came first to the sepulchre. And he stooping down, and looking in, saw the linen clothes lying; yet went he not in. Then cometh Simon Peter following him, and went into the sepulchre, and seeth the linen clothes lie. And the napkin, what was about his head, not lying with the linen clothes, but wrapped together in a place by itself.' The other three gospels, all of which tell of the stone rolled back and of Mary Magdalene discovering the body's disappearance, do not refer to the grave clothes. Yet the mention made of it by John clearly gives the Shroud Biblical proof.

What secular proof do we have? Ian Wilson spent years gathering evidence and had made a number of speculative yet plausible connections. He had read history at Oxford and was working as promotions and publicity manager for the *Bristol Evening Post* and its associated newspapers. He had been fascinated by the Shroud for almost twenty years; since 1966 he had been led deeper and deeper into research intended originally for nothing more than a short article, a pot boiler. In 1974 he was accepted into Catholicism, his wife's faith, converted from his lifelong agnosticism.

Wilson's thesis is that the Holy Shroud of Turin was in fact the Mandylion or Image of Edessa. From the tenth to the thirteenth centuries, this was one of the principal treasures of Byzantium, that fabled centre of relics and wonders. In the tenth century, it had been brought by the Byzantine army from the city of Edessa, where it had been on occasional display for four hundred years. It had been found in the sixth century, hidden in a niche in the city wall; what was more plausible than to suppose it had been there all along? And it had been carefully secreted because, during the second half of the first century, King

Ma'nu VI of Edessa had championed the ancient paganism of his people and persecuted those who sought to drive it out. His victims were mainly Christians one of whose earliest churches in Asia Minor was established in Edessa.

The Christian community flourished there so early because, it was said, Ma'nu's father, Abgar V, had been miraculously cured of his disease. One of the original seventy disciples of Jesus (He had said to them, 'I send you forth as lambs among wolves') had travelled to Edessa in answer to an appeal sent by the King, after Jesus's Crucifixion. The disciple had brought with him a gift, a 'portrait' of Jesus. With this in his possession, Abgar had been cured of his sickness. It seemed more than likely – to Wilson, it was virtually certain – that this miraculous likeness had been the Image found hidden in the city wall.

What, however, connected the Image of Edessa, the famous Mandylion of Constantinople, with the much later Shroud of Turin? Wilson turned to a study of iconography. The arrival of the Image in Byzantium from Edessa ended the confusion that had previously existed among painters as to the lineaments of Christ's face. A uniformity of portraiture was then established which has never since been challenged. From the variety of concepts which inspired earlier artists, a single one emerged: from picture after picture there looked out the same long-cheeked face, fork-bearded, framed by long hair and often bearing mysterious marks – marks we can see today in the blood-stains borne by the man of the Shroud. If that new artistic uniformity was not based on what the Mandylion revealed, and if the Mandylion in turn was not a face on the Shroud, then coincidences on an astonishing scale had occurred across the centuries.

Early in the thirteenth century, the Mandylion vanished. Like many other Byzantine relics, it had disappeared during the sacking of that incomparable city by the furious Crusaders in 1204. In the 1350s, the Holy Shroud went, for the first time, on public display, at Lirey, in France. If Mandylion and Shroud were indeed the same, where had it been in the meantime? According to Wilson it was that mysterious bearded head said to have been revered for nearly a century by the Knights Templars. It was put on show, he points out, by Jeanne de Vergy, the widow of a famous soldier, Geoffrey de Charny, killed at Poitiers. During Philip the Fair's extermination of the Templars in 1314, a Geoffrey de Charny was burned in the same fire as the Grand Master. Conformity of spelling was not a fourteenth-century virtue; it is true, nevertheless, that Wilson could establish no connection between the two men except a similarity of pronunciation. Were they of the same family? Was the Shroud in that family's possession? Had it been preserved when the Templars were destroyed? No one can say. It is one of the weaker links in the chain – although it is a link.

From that first exposition in Lirey onwards, the history of the Shroud is clear. In the fifteenth century, it passed to the Dukes of Savoy. In 1532, it was scorched in a fire, and two years later was patched by nuns; both the damage and the repairs can still clearly be seen. Later that century, the Shroud was moved from Chambéry to Turin, where it has been ever since. Wilson has since written in extended and fascinating detail his theory in *The Turin Shroud* (Gollancz in Britain, Doubleday in the United States), which is absolutely required reading for anyone with a real interest in the background and authenticity of the Shroud.

Wilson's early script also challenged modern science to settle once and for all the genuineness of this mysterious relic. Science, of course, cannot actually authenticate such an object. It can only set a series of tests, failure at any one of which demolishes its claims. Success proves only that it has passed untarnished this *single* examination – tomorrow's quite different analysis may prove it spurious. All one can say is that, with each successive positive result, the likelihood of authenticity becomes greater.

One long-established fact, rightly made much of in the

script, is the astonishing nature of the image itself: it is like a photographic negative. This was realised in 1898 when the Shroud was photographed by an Italian lawyer, the noted amateur photographer, Secondo Pia. Only when he lifted his full-plate glass negative from the developing fluid did Pia grasp its significance. White on black, he had before him a true image of the man on the shroud – the true image, as Pia was profoundly convinced, of Jesus Christ. He stared at it with a mixture of awe, reverence and curiosity. If what he believed was true, he was the first man in two millenia to see the actual lines and planes of that extraordinary face, the exact proportions of that tortured body, so clearly human, so necessarily divine. Later, and much clearer, photographs, taken in 1931 by Giuseppe Enrie, confirm and amplify what Secondo Pia first established.

Wilson proposed to bring medical evidence explaining the exact nature of the wounds displayed by the Shroud image. In his first script, he included testimony from Dr David Willis, a Somerset general practitioner long interested in the subject. It is to Dr Willis, who died not long before its publication, that Wilson's book is dedicated. Wilson also faced and discounted some explanations that had been offered for the creation of the image, notably that it had been formed by contact with the body. As he wrote in his Presenter's narration, many attempts have been made to reproduce this effect. 'The results have, without exception, been grotesque and deformed.' In all this, he was following research that had, as we shall see, already been done on the Shroud. He also gave his support, however, to what is still a very speculative theory – that the negative image on that ancient strip of linen was some kind of scorch mark, burned into and so a part of the cloth. He turned for evidence to the 'shadows' left by the living as they died instantly in the cataclysmic flames of Hiroshima and Nagasaki. He wrote, 'Is it not therefore conceivable that at the moment of resurrection the process of Jesus's body passing through the Shroud was something closely akin to the release of atomic energy? Perhaps a flash of light so powerful that the image … was literally burned onto the cloth, in different intensities of shading according to distance, with the blood-clots being reliquified and "fossilised" into the linen at the same time?'

With this wealth of detail and this welter of speculation before him, it is no wonder that David Rolfe read and reread, gripped more and more relentlessly by the conviction not only that he had found the basis for a film he could make but that it was one he *would* make. He would himself find the finance, bring together the technicians, arrange the locations, supervise the shooting script, hire the necessary actors, pick the right voice to read the narration. He felt with unshakable and increasing certainty that he had found the venture for which he was looking.

CHAPTER TWO

The first task of a producer with an idea is to raise the money to realise it on film. In the world of moving pictures, where everything else is insubstantial – talent, imagination, information, words, images and music – finance is the one demanding link with hard reality. People can become millionaires through backing films – and millionaires can sometimes become people. It has been both the curse and the blessing of film-making that it has always been relatively so expensive: a blessing because it winnows out the less determined; a curse because it attracts those with nothing to offer except money. It has made of the creation of filmed dramas and documentaries an industry, dominated by people who think like industrialists. Yet even for the most idealistic, some element in the glamour of making movies derives from precisely the factor they most abhor – that it involves large, sometimes huge, sums of money.

David Rolfe determined very early that if he were to make the film at all, it would have to be comprehensive, visually interesting and accessible to non-expert, non-religious audiences. He determined neither to convert nor to preach to the converted. That meant adopting a neutral tone, never running ahead of the evidence, never assuming anything that had not been proved or could be taken as indisputably true. Wilson's script called for shooting in the various relevant locations – Lirey and Chambéry in France, Turin in Italy, Edessa (now Urfa) and Istanbul in Turkey, as well perhaps as the Holy Land. David agreed with this plan; they would have to film in all the places where the Shroud, and the earlier Mandylion, had been exposed. The original script seemed very static; too many experts spoke to the camera, the presenter appeared rather obtrusive, there was not enough direct action. Wherever possible, it would have to be dramatised. All these decisions involved spending money. Even before he began work in earnest, David knew that he was undertaking a documentary much more expensive than the common run. It seemed that if he were going into independent production, he was going with something of a splash.

First of all he pared down his activities, retaining only those projects necessary to keep himself in funds; he wanted to maintain the new venture's momentum. In Bristol, Ian Wilson was rewriting his script, ironing out the over-reverential tone, which not only assumed the Shroud was in fact that of Jesus but was calculated to produce an unfavourable reaction in those less committed than he to Christian orthodoxy.

These were all matters within David's control. When he approached financiers, however, his whole project came to a halt. No film or television company, no independent producer, no bank, no dispenser of risk capital, could see what he saw in this investigation he proposed. Nor could he devote all his time to it – indeed, for the first few months, he could do nothing at all directly. He flew out to Dubhai for another sponsored film – he had, after all, his living to earn.

Soon after his return to London, however, he was approached by a man prepared to put up the necessary money. He was the owner of a photographic processing firm for whom the peculiar negative quality of the Shroud might well have seemed a possible source of publicity. At the last moment, however, it became clear that he was imposing conditions David found impossible to accept; they involved, among other things, the loss of David's own company, which this man wanted to take over. It was becoming clear that the raising of capital was going to be more difficult than he had originally anticipated.

It was at this juncture, with success looking increasingly unlikely, that he offered to buy a year's option on the film rights to Wilson's work. Until then, no money had actually changed hands, and this seems perhaps a curious moment to have chosen to do so. David had, however, a good reason for it. The conditions imposed by the would-be backer, including, as they did, full control over the production, might be unacceptable to him, but Wilson might well find them reasonable. He gave his collaborator the details of the offer, adding that 'if they are able to raise the necessary finance, it is only fair to allow you to decide how you want [the film] to be produced'. It was his offer, however, that Wilson chose to accept. David would hold the film rights until the autumn of 1976. His own money now committed – no great sum, but then he did not have much – he set out grimly to do battle once more in the financial wars.

The next phase contained an element of farce. It involved a collection of grave city gentlemen accepting at face value a North American operator who not only did not have the money he said he had but also did not have it in the bank he claimed to own. The claim, of course, was genuine; it was the bank which was not. Suspicious at last, it was David rather than one of the experts who decided to give the Fraud Squad a speculative telephone call.

'You realise that we can't tell you anything, sir', a careful voice explained. 'We can't give out information to members of the public.' There was a pause, then the voice went on, in slightly lowered tones. 'The only thing I will say, sir, is this – it was a wise move on your part to give us a ring.' With this cryptic warning, offered in the true spirit of British compromise, David had to be content; and indeed it was enough to chill the blood of anyone in his position. He had been relying on these largely benign financiers. He had been the animating spirit in organising them into a steering committee charged with raising the finances his project needed. From the director of that notional bank the committee had received a letter stating categorically 'that we are prepared to finance the production of the film in question'. It had seemed as if his major barrier had crumbled away.

Worse was yet to come. Now it was the Fraud Squad who telephoned him: would he please pay them a visit? The following day he found himself confronted not only by the Metropolitan Police but also the FBI. His putative guarantor had been, it seemed, under intercontinental surveillance. He was, the detectives told him, involved in the forging of gold bullion certificates; his 'bank' did not exist beyond its name and headed notepaper. His involvement with David's steering committee had almost certainly had only one purpose: to establish him as a person well-thought of by the respectable and the genuinely wealthy. The police asked David if, for a little while, he would remain on friendly terms with the man, keep him talking, keep him making promises. They would have officers close by, should intervention become necessary. They would be grateful if he later passed on to them anything the man had said. Reluctantly, David agreed. He felt that what he was doing was a long way from producing a film, and even further from everything the Shroud represented.

Over lunch, however, as the rolling promises broke over him like Atlantic breakers, his patience snapped. 'You'll never do any of this,' he said, tersely. 'I don't believe what you tell me any more. You'll do none of it!' He got up from the table and walked away. It was only two years later, with his film finally finished and being prepared for its first showing, that he tried to find out what had happened to his self-confident 'benefactor'. He had been deported from Britain to face charges for company fraud in his homeland. The forgeries, however, were never the subject of a prosecution; lack of evidence had thwarted the police.

The effect of this small adventure was extremely depressing. The steering committee broke up – almost, it seems, from embarrassment rather than any more practical reason. All the work that had been put in, all the meetings, the lunches, the letters written and minutes circulated, had been in vain. Hopes had yet again to be furled. David was once more at the beginning – with the difference that now the option he had bought from Ian Wilson was running out. The cost of making the film had been estimated, during steering committee meetings, at close to £150,000. Though still making money on other projects, David was running an overdraft sanctioned by his admirably co-operative and understanding bank. He had so far spent some £3000 of his own company's money on the venture. Yet he seemed further from that magical day when the camera would turn than he had ever been.

Nevertheless, his belief in the film remained absolutely firm. He showed that by the visit he made to Dr Max Frei.

Dr Frei turned his wide biological knowledge and his skill with the microscope into a major branch of criminology. In 1948 he was a founder of the Scientific Service formed to aid the Criminal Police of his native Zurich; four years later he began lecturing on criminology at the city's university. The information he could elicit from a single dust sample might run to many closely-written pages and provide vital evidence. He had published many works, the bulk of them on the application of microscopy to criminal investigation, and, with his background as a student of botany, he was an expert in the distribution and variety of pollens. Dr Frei had nominally retired in 1972, but, a sinewy and sprightly man, was much in demand as a consultant and independent expert by police departments both in and outside Switzerland.

His name was first connected with investigations into the Shroud in the report issued by the Commission of Examination set up in 1969 by the ecclesiastical authorities in Turin. In 1955 he had published an article on the falsification of photographs; now he was among the experts called to testify before a notary that pictures taken of the Shroud did not 'show any element or trace of retouching or anomalous presence which would invalidate their genuineness'. While helping to authenticate these prints and negatives, however, 'with the aim of ascertaining their perfect correspondence with the original', he had seen something arousing his deeper investigative instincts: on the surface of this extraordinary cloth, and in the tiny crevices between the threads, lay particles the secrets of which he knew how to reveal – dust.

With the permission of Cardinal Pellegrino, who had organised the examination, Max Frei took his samples. He has a special method for doing so: he lays an especially clear adhesive tape down so that any dust in the area covered will adhere to the glue, then he takes it carefully off and folds it, glue against glue. This traps his samples in an almost totally transparent envelope, both preserving them and making them available for examination. With a tiny punch he can even select individual elements when he wants to examine these under greater magnification.

Under the microscope Frei discovered in his samples all the debris he had come to expect. Most were of no immediate use: very little can be made of tiny mineral particles or shreds of plant fibre. What he isolated and concentrated on were the spores of pollen that he found. Making sense of these was first a question of identification and then one of statistics. Once it was known which spores were present, their numbers became significant. A single spore might mean no more than that a freak wind long ago had carried it an unexpected distance; several, and of several geographically related varieties, pointed to exposure in a particular location and, if the vegetation had altered, at a particular time. For under the electron microscope, pollen spores from different plant varieties prove to have absolutely distinct characteristics, as individual as crystal structures or fingerprints. They do not deteriorate with age, their outer skins being so resistant that they can survive over thousands, even millions of years. For the investigator, their only drawback is their small size – down to 1/100th of a millimeter. With this problem Frei had learned to cope, partly by devising new techniques of his own.

His discoveries were not, in the first months of 1976, by

any means complete. There were many varieties of pollen that he had not been able to identify, others which took the known story no further – those the Shroud would have picked up during its exposures in France and Italy – and others again that might have meant something two thousand years ago, when the species they derived from had been confined to particular localities, but which have today been spread by Man to many different parts of the world. Nevertheless, his early results were encouraging. He had found pollens that belonged in Asia Minor, and one or two specimens from the Holy Land. What he wanted to do now was to travel to those places and examine the local plants in order to see how many of the unidentified pollens fell into these Eastern Mediterranean categories.

David had come across Max Frei's name in a press cutting from a Houston paper. It had been sent to him by a Texas businessman whom he had met a year earlier in Riyadh, the Saudi Arabian capital. Since first reading the Ian Wilson script he had made a point of mentioning the Shroud to almost everyone he met; it was a broadcast scattering of seed which had now borne fruit. Excited to see the itinerary Wilson had proposed for the Shroud supported by this unexpected evidence, he wrote to Dr Frei. He wanted to make sure that these investigations would be, as were Ian Wilson's carefully worked-out theories, exclusively his to film. Early in May, 1976, he and Dr Frei met, with cinematic brevity, at Zurich Airport. David could not offer a fee for the necessary filming, but he could offer the travel facilities Dr Frei needed to complete his work. On the basis that David's company would underwrite his expenses during his Middle Eastern journeys, in addition to the fee, Dr Frei agreed to become one of David's growing team. With his enthusiasm for the project, he proved to be a valuable addition.

In the search for finance David now turned to a new possibility. Wilson had had some contact with the Holy Shroud Guild of America and, using this for leverage, David now approached them. A letter from Wilson to Father Finaldi, the Guild's vice-president, helped to open negotiations. The Guild learned for the first time of Dr Frei's work in these early letters. It was a fact that helped to endow David and his project with the right air of efficiency and seriousness. Father Rinaldi began to search for possible investors; in a matter of weeks he let David know that he had found one: a wealthy mid-Western Catholic industrialist who had in the past supported religious causes and ventures, and had responded with some interest to the Guild's overtures. His name was Harry John, his headquarters were in Milwaukee – and he wanted to meet David Rolfe there as soon as possible.

For David, the situation was becoming desperate. His option on the film rights had only a few more weeks to run, his credit was almost at an end, he had aroused interest in many potential backers, without bringing one of them to the point of actually shouldering any responsibility. If he spent more money on a trip to the United States and Harry John turned out as shy, nervous or fraudulent as so many others had been, he would have come in every sense to the end of his resources. Yet it was too late for caution. Unless he managed to arrange something in the immediate future, he would have little future left to arrange anything in. Taking a deep breath, he plunged even deeper into debt and, for the first time in his life, crossed the Atlantic.

The first revelation was the character of Father Rinaldi. David says of him, 'He was the closest that I have ever met to a living saint'. For many years a parish priest in an outlying, predominantly Italian suburb of New York, he was the centre of a developed and thriving religious life, popular with his parishioners, officiating in an ornate church before crowded congregations, the symbol and preserver of a deep-rooted Christianity perhaps increasingly rare in the modern world. He had established in his Corpus Christi Church a shrine to the Holy Shroud said to be unique in North America. At its centre stood a full-size illuminated transparency of the frontal aspect of the Shroud image. Yet he retained the intellectual and spiritual honesty that drew him to support investigations of all kinds into this baffling and mysterious cloth. As David talked with Father Rinaldi, as he realised his openness of mind and generosity of spirit, as he saw how pleased the people who knew him best always were to see him, he felt his own long-established prejudices softening. He still thought the Church almost entirely a mass of ancient nonsense – but if it had people like Father Rinaldi in it, it was not as valueless as he had thought.

The President of the Guild, Father Otterbein, provided something of a contrast. His path led him to a fierce guardianship of the Guild's – and, by extension, the Church's – finances and integrity. It made him perhaps less immediately appealing, but his function no less essential. He put David through a fierce spell of questioning, finally thawing as the satisfactory answers piled up. With these meetings and journeying successfully over, the time had come to meet the unknown millionaire whose sponsorship might save the project.

A car brought the little deputation from the Plaza Hotel, where they were staying, to the low, slightly forbidding, modern office block on the outskirts of Milwaukee from which Harry John ran his business. In an impersonal reception area they went through the rigmarole of a security-conscious age: wrote their names, their places of origin and their addresses and submitted to having a photograph taken. Finally cleared, they were taken to the upper floor and ushered in to the comfort of the building's most important office. A lady came in, charming, middle-aged, friendly, evidently Italian: Mrs John. She had heard of Father Rinaldi and seemed delighted to meet him; then she turned to David. 'What is it you actually intend to do?' she asked.

For days, for weeks, David had been preparing the

speech that would finally unlock the finances he needed. Now, like a gun with a hair trigger, this slight stimulus set him off. He launched into his statement of intent, fluent, precise yet, indiscernably to the others, out of control. After ten minutes or so of what was, perhaps, a slightly misdirected lecture, the sounding of a buzzer abruptly halted him. Mrs John smiled. 'Harry will be here in a moment.'

Silence followed this. Nervousness redoubled. Rigid with tension, David watched the door. It opened; anti-climatically, a man who might have been some attendant devoted to the maintenance of the building wandered in. His trousers hung baggily about him, his feet showed through the gaps in a pair of plastic sandals, he was unshaven. Only when Mrs John announced her husband and began the introductions did David realise that he was finally face-to-face with the millionaire.

'Well, Mr Rolfe – what have you come to tell us?" Response remained automatic. David set out a second time on the same speech, hearing himself repeat almost word for word what he had said only a few minutes earlier. And at almost exactly the same point, he was stopped again.

'Time for Mass', said Harry John. Everyone trooped downstairs to where, like a feudal baron or an eighteenth century aristocrat, the industrialist had built a private chapel. There were a few new faces in the congregation, notably those of the young John boys. At the end of the service – David's first experience of Catholic ritual – it was Harry John's custom to have everyone shake everyone else's hand, uttering as they did so the words, 'Peace be with you'. David's adaptation of this formula to a labour-saving 'The same to you', brought the children out in fierce giggles. Harry John, having paid enough lip-service to the ideal of peace, returned to practicalities by cracking their impudent heads together.

In the house next door, David joined the others for a vegetarian lunch. Seeds of various kinds – sunflower, sesame and so on – were supplemented by a broth based on orange juice. After the pleasant and nourishing meal, everyone returned to the office – everyone, that is, except the host. For an hour they waited, keeping a desultory conversation going, before Harry John returned. He had just ordered ten thousand plastic bags, emblazoned with a slogan suitable for the eucharistic conference for which they were destined.

'Are you a Catholic, Mr Rolfe?' he asked.

David said that he was not.

'Then what are you?'

'I'm an agnostic.'

Harry John looked somewhat taken aback. David, close to desperation, nevertheless said stoutly that he had no intention of making a religious film. 'What interests me, as an agnostic, is the fact that we're dealing with historical and – if we remember Dr Frei – scientific evidence. It's on that that we'll have to base any claim for the authenticity of the Shroud. And if we base everything on the evidence, we'll have no need to go in for propaganda.'

Even as he spoke, knowing at the same time that there was nothing else he could have said, he had the strong feeling that his five-thousand-mile journey had been in vain. Surely whatever chance they may have been to persuade Harry John to finance the film had just been destroyed. The millionaire, an extremely religious man, did not seem the sort who would let such facts speak for themselves.

When the group left an hour or so later, nothing had been decided. David was pessimistic; Father Rinaldi much less so, believing that they would get the funds that they had come for. He had always felt a special attachment to the Shroud, from the moment when, as a choirboy in Turin Cathedral, he had been reprimanded for making too much noise in the chapel where it was kept. 'What is the Shroud, Father?', he had asked the offended priest, and the old man had taken him and the other boys aside and told them its astonishing story. Now he felt that his long fascination with the Shroud and everything that appertained to it would not permit this latest venture to founder. So the priest comforted the agnostic as best he could.

It was in a depressed frame of mind, nevertheless, that David flew back to Britain. His money was exhausted. He had tried every possibility. Now it seemed that his final effort had again failed. And this disappointment, so late in the day, was more bitter than the others. He had no more resilience left nor any time in which to fight back. This black mood lasted almost a week – lasted, that is, until a letter from the Guild arrived to tell him that Harry John, unconcerned with his agnosticism, had agreed. The necessary money was at last available. Father Rinaldi's optimism had been vindicated.

CHAPTER THREE

With the money now available, David Rolfe could begin the real work of production. He could renew his option with Ian Wilson; he could bind Dr Frei, not only with the usual retainer, but also by seriously planning the proposed Middle Eastern tour; he could contemplate combining the criminologist's journey with a reconnaissance of his own. First, however, he wanted to assure himself of the film's scientific base. He already had the early testimony of Dr Frei, with the promise of more to come. But he had heard from Father Rinaldi that at the Air Force Academy at Colorado Springs, USA, certain scientists – he did not know in which disciplines – had been working with photographs of the Shroud obtained from the Guild. David wrote to them asking about their research. He knew, too, that there had been an authorised investigation of the Shroud under the auspices of the diocese of Turin, in 1973. It was the preliminaries that Dr Frei had attended in 1969 as photographic expert. The results of the 1973 investigation had, however, been published only in Italian. David commissioned a translation.

The Silent Witness was beginning to act as a sort of catalyst in the world-wide activity that surrounded the Shroud. Because of it, work was being done that would not have been done otherwise; because of it, experts who would have made no contact with each other were being brought together. Dr Frei's work had been added to support Ian Wilson's theories, for example; and Father Rinaldi's attention had then been brought to it. Now that the film was under way, too, the Vatican began to take an interest; Monsignor Ricci, a man who had made a lifetime study of the Shroud (albeit from a standpoint so determinedly and even narrowly Catholic as to lead him to conclusions outsiders usually considered rather fanciful), now made contact with David. This seemed less surprising when it became known that he was an acquaintance of, and much respected by, the film's present sponsor, Harry John. There was no question, however, but that a new energy was stirring the small world of Shroud studies. *The Silent Witness*, before a single foot of it had even been shot, had already quickened the development of knowledge about this famous sheet of linen.

Once the photographs taken by Secondo Pia had, as it were, solidified the image so mistily visible on the Shroud itself, turning that mysterious negative into a positive demanding further study, the scientific community began to take notice of it. Perhaps to say 'scientific community' exaggerates the response; the face is, nonetheless, that scientists of some repute ventured to investigate what had hitherto been the exclusive province of historians, theologians and the devoutly faithful. It could, therefore, be said that the work being stimulated, co-ordinated and even sponsored by David Rolfe as he strove to make his film had its roots in analyses attempted decades earlier.

One reason for this was that when they were originally published Pia's photographs stirred rather than stilled the controversy that surrounded the Shroud. Sceptics retained their doubts; those who believed in the relic's authenticity had their convictions confirmed. Thus an anonymous witness, a 'well-known archaeologist and painter' who saw the photographs, exclaimed, 'Either this is the authentic Shroud, or it is God who has painted it!' The newspaper *Corriere Nazionale* proclaimed, 'The Redeemer ... reappeared on the glass miraculously outlined, with an amazing fineness of detail ... In short, after nineteen hundred years, during which the world contemplated the figure of the Nazarene by the aid of tradition, the photograph of the Shroud has now given us a picture'. But others insisted that Pia had done no more than bring out paint that had faded beyond the perception of the naked eye or that some unspecified process in the photography itself – the technology of which was still mysterious to most people – was responsible. To Pia's consternation, there were also various voices suggesting that he had contrived his results, that he had tampered with and retouched the negatives. This was a peculiarly unpleasant accusation, for Pia had made it a point of principle never artificially to sharpen up or improve his pictures in the darkroom.

Ever since the Shroud had been exhibited in Europe during the fourteenth century, there had of course been many who doubted its authenticity. One of the earliest had been Pierre d'Arcis, who was Bishop of Troyes when, in 1389, the Shroud was shown in public for the second time. This had been at the instigation of yet another Geoffrey de Charny, the son of the original exhibitor, and it was an event that outraged the Bishop. He considered it a blatant fraud and wrote in the bluntest possible terms to the Avignon Pope, Clement VII. Thirty years before, he pointed out, his predecessor in the bishopric had faced the same problem when Jeanne de Vergy had first displayed the controversial relic – 'a certain cloth', as the Bishop dismissively described it. That earlier Bishop of Troyes, Henri, had, 'after diligent inquiry and investigation ... discovered the fraud and how the said cloth had been cunningly painted, the truth being attested by the artist who had painted it, to wit, that it was the work of human skill, and not miraculously wrought or bestowed ... I cannot fully or sufficiently express in writing the grievous nature of the scandal'.

As a matter of fact, the Bishop was unable to persuade Clement to rescind the permission he had already given to the Abbey of Lirey to display the Shroud. All the Pope was prepared to do was to insist that the monks, and their sponsor, Margaret de Charny, should not state explicitly that their image had been directly created in any way by the body of Jesus. They should take care to warn the public that it was only a 'figure or representation'. Nevertheless, upon the Bishop of Troyes' convictions five hundred years before, twentieth-century scholars, savants and experts in mediaeval history continued to base their own. What was the evidence of a mere photograph compared with that of the authentic letter from Pierre d'Arcis? He had said that it had been proved that the Shroud was a forgery; he had said that there was an artist who had painted it and confessed to having done so (or – such are the ambiguities of Latin – that there was an artist, an expert painter, who had testified that the picture on the Shroud was the work of human hands). Bishop d'Arcis had been there at the time and what he said was, therefore, the most likely to be true. Thus supported, the sceptics rallied. The interest that had for a while been excited in the Shroud waned. It seemed as though it would become again one more relic among thousands, venerated by the convinced but disregarded by everyone else. Science, however, was about to rescue, for once, the certainties of the religious.

In 1902, Paul Vignon published a book, *The Shroud of Christ*, based on his examination of it in conjunction with Pia's photographs. 'The results of this study lasting over a year and a half', he wrote in his Introduction, 'are what we place today before the public. They appeal not only to the archaeologists and students in the laboratory, but also to the world of Art, and to those who are interested in facts which bear upon the foundations of our modern society. Our researches have been carried on without prejudice, and with equal respect to the claims of conflicting beliefs.'

Vignon was wealthy, intelligent, courageous, a polymath of the sort more common then than now. He was an accomplished mountaineer, having to his credit a number of hazardous Alpine first ascents; he was a skilled painter who had exhibited in the salons of Paris; and he was a dauntingly competent biologist who worked as principal assistant to Professor Delage, a scientist who taught at the Sorbonne and was also a director of the

Museum of Natural History. It was, in fact, Delage who had first showed Vignon the photographs of the Shroud. Both men were excited by them and uncertain what to think. None of the available explanations seemed quite adequate. It was because of this sense of intellectual unease that Vignon decided to investigate further: if the Shroud were not authentic, he was confident that he would be able to demonstrate how the forger had created it.

Sensibly beginning with the basic facts, he travelled to Turin and spoke with Secondo Pia. His impressions of that lawyer-photographer, and one or two corroborative prints of pictures taken more recently by other people, convinced him that the photographs were genuine. If there had been a forger at work, it had not been Pia. Vignon would be able to rely on the photographs, at least.

The most important fact about the photographs was their demonstration that the Shroud image was a negative. The second most important fact was the amount of detail they showed. Vignon put these two together. If the artist, the 'forger', had in fact painted the image in negative, he would in a sense have been working blind. He would not have been able to see what he was doing. How then could he have included so much fine detail? It would have been a superhuman task.

What if a simple colour reversal, not unknown in paintings centuries old, had turned the image into a negative? The objection here was once again the detail; a picture in such a state of disrepair would not have retained so many fine particularities. And if it had deteriorated, it must have been very bright and attractive when first displayed fresh from the forger's brush. Had no one noticed this at the time? On the other hand, if one wanted to avoid that problem, could one actually paint an image on linen as faint and wispy, as devoid of outline, as the one on the Shroud? Vignon put his own skills to use, trying to create a replica of the figure, first with oil paints, then with water colours. It proved almost impossible to paint even the crudest approximation of the real image; when he had finally done so, nothing would keep it on the linen. Once the cloth was folded, the picture simply peeled away.

If the image had not been painted, had it perhaps been created by pressure? Had the lineaments of face and body somehow been pressed into the cloth? Vignon decided to experiment, with himself as subject. He tells us, without embellishment, 'The writer lay down on an operating table, and his face was carefully smeared with red chalk. The same thing had been done with a false beard which was fixed on to his face ...' The scene this conjures up must have been one of the most bizarre in the annals of science: the red-faced Vignon, false beard bristling, lying on the table like some monstrosity out of a horror story; his two serious attendants, men of integrity and honour, administrators in the Sorbonne bureaucracy, approaching him, a cloth held ready. Slowly they cover that ghastly crimson head; their hands smooth the white linen against the contours of the face; under their fingers the body lies still, unprotesting, as though actually dead; perhaps the false beard, thrust aside, protrudes for a moment; perhaps, for a moment, the closed eyelids flicker. Almost reverently, the men lift the cloth, their movements slow, careful. They hold it up. On the table the corpse stirs. With smeared red face and unconvincing beard awry, the man looks at his confederates, then at the cloth. He sighs, lies back. 'Again', he says, closing his eyes. 'Try it again.'

The results of these experiments, reproduced in Vignon's book, look sinister and disturbing. Detail is smeared, features are displaced. The cheeks appear grotesquely distended, the lips turned inside out and flattened, the eyes flow down towards the nostrils: these are images that seem likely to be accompanied by the signature of Francis Bacon. Nothing further from the ghostly precision of the figure on the Shroud can be imagined. Vignon wrote, 'One thing seems certain, if the forger at the Abbey of Lirey had been reduced to work in the way we did, he would never have obtained a portrait which could stand photography. On the Shroud, if the features are faint in places, the proportions remain admirable; and the powerful effect they produce is mainly due to the perfect harmony which they present as a whole ... At the same time, if the forger had obtained a head no better than those in our illustration he would probably have been quite content with that result, bad as it is. His work would not have been criticised so long as no photographic camera led to an investigation of it.'

Having eliminated to his own satisfaction such methods as may have been immediately available to a forger, Vignon now wanted to establish how the Shroud image actually had been created. If the agency had not been human, it must have been natural. He set himself to study its characteristics. One fact had already struck him – the image had come into being even in those areas where the body cannot have been touching the cloth. In other words, there had been an effect at a distance, suggesting that some form of emanation may have caused the image. With the body in its cave tomb, Vignon thought, this was unlikely to have been light. Much more plausible was the suggestion that it had been some form of chemical vapour. But could a chemical vapour have caused such an image?

Working with Professor René Colson, an expert in the action of such vapours, Vignon set up various experiments. For example, he and Colson covered a plaster cast of a head with zinc powder and placed it in a box impenetrable to light. They then put beside it a glass photographic plate, in such a way that the plaster-cast's forehead, nose and beard were actually touching it. They then shut the box tightly and left it for twenty-four hours. When they opened it again, there on the plate was a faint but clearly discernable image. In character it was very similar to that of the Shroud. Had they solved this centuries-old mystery?

Their next problem was to decide what chemical agency might have caused the necessary vapours in the Shroud's case and whether such an agency would in fact have created the desired effect. In the Gospel of St John they found, 'And after this, Joseph of Arimathaea, being a disciple of Jesus, but secretly for fear of the Jews, besought Pilate that he might take away the body of Jesus: and Pilate gave him leave. He came therefore, and took the body of Jesus. And there came also Nicodemus, which at the first came to Jesus by night, and brought a mixture of myrrh and aloes ... Then took they the body of Jesus, and wound it in linen clothes with the spices, as the manner of the Jews is to bury ...'

Research told them that 'the manner of the Jews to bury' involved pounding up a mixture of myrrh and aloes in pure olive oil. Vignon proposed that it was this, soaking into the linen, that had made the cloth sensitive to some form of vapour. What he did not know was, what kind of vapour could it have been? Certainly ammonia, present in the body, gave off a vapour. Would that cause an image to appear on linen saturated with their specially prepared funerary spices? They tried it with the plaster cast of a hand and were almost too successful. They had to damp down the exudation with a kid glove. Would there, however, have been ammonia spread over the body in such a way as to leave so detailed and complete an imprint on the Shroud? Where would it have come from?

They pondered this and soon arrived at an answer. Ammonia was found in the urea in the body; this came to the surface when one sweated and in greater quantities when one was in pain or terror. The man of the Shroud had been in pain for several days and had died in agony. Whoever he had been, that was plain from the evidence of his wounds and scars. Clearly, the naked body must have shone with perspiration. When brought at last to the dark rest of the nearby tomb, he must still have been covered with a thin film of sweat, and thus of the ammonia which was one of its elements. From the evidence of the blood, he had not been washed: as St Luke says of Joseph of Arimathaea, 'This man went unto Pilate, and begged the body of Jesus. And he took it down, and wrapped it in linen, and laid it in a sepulchre ... And that day was the preparation, and the sabbath drew on. And the women also, which came with him from Gallilee, followed after, and beheld the sepulchre, and how his body was laid. And they returned, and prepared spices and ointments; and rested the sabbath day according to the commandment. Now upon the first day of the week, very early in the morning, they came unto the sepulchre, bringing the spices which they had prepared ... And they found the stone rolled away from the sepulchre.'

Having solved to his own satisfaction the mystery of how the image on the Shroud had been created, Vignon tackled the perhaps more perplexing question: was it the body of Jesus that it portrayed? It was Vignon who first noted the correspondences between the story suggested by the image and that to be found in the Gospels. The Biblical account told that 'one of the soldiers with a spear pierced his side, and forthwith came there out blood and water'; below the ribs, sure enough, one could see signs of that wound. St Mark describes how the soldiers – or perhaps the Hebrew crowd – 'plaited a crown of thorns, and put it about his head'; on the scalp of the Shroud figure were the lacerations one might have expected. Above all, there were the wounds of the crucifixion itself – although the man of the Shroud had been nailed, not through the palms as so many paintings had over the centuries demonstrated, but through the wrists. It was Vignon who first pointed out that the hands would never bear the weight of the whole body: anyone thus nailed up would simply tear the flesh from the metal. Despite the artistic tradition, it was the Shroud's nails through the wrist that made the only anatomical sense. It was Vignon, too, who first made a close examination of the marks of flagellation that scored the figure's back, buttocks and legs. He asserted that no painter, and no forger either, could have produced such a complex network of injuries. As to the scars themselves, he matched enough of them to the lashes of a Roman *flagrum* to show how they must have been inflicted.

Vignon produced at this stage two further arguments against the figure's having been the creation of a mediaeval painter. The first was the man's nudity. No painter, or even forger, in the fourteenth century would have depicted Jesus without clothes. Representations of the Shroud itself falsify the figure by wrapping it in a loincloth. And then there was the other factor – the man can have lain in the cloth for only a short while. There were no signs of physical corruption. In that Middle Eastern climate, even in spring, it is often fairly warm. No body would last, in fact, for more than a very few days. Whoever had been wrapped in that length of linen had not remained very long where he was. This matched the Bible story: if it were to be believed, Jesus's corpse had vanished over the Passover weekend.

It was Delage, the senior of the two men, who presented these findings to the French Academy. Vignon was among the two hundred people who crowded into the hall to hear the dissertation. Under the ceiling where the voices of the famous dead still faintly reverberated – Daguerre introducing photography, Pasteur his vaccines – Delage laid out the results of the long, painstaking investigation he and, more especially, Vignon had undertaken. At the end of his lecture he stated unequivocally, 'The man of the Shroud is the Christ!' In England, the *Lancet* seemed to accept this thesis, as did the *Times*. *Nature* wrote a neutral piece on the research, and *Scientific American* copied the article. Yet there were many of his colleagues who openly jeered at Delage and the conclusions he had endorsed. They accused him of not behaving scientifically. Knowing he had always been at most an agnostic, and probably an atheist, they said that now he had had a sudden rush of religion to the head. They said that the work he and Vignon had done was very far from being conclusive.

Delage replied with a statement that remains relevant, both to Shroud studies and all similar specialities. 'I willingly recognise that none of these arguments offer the features of an irrefutable demonstration; but it must be recognised that their whole constitutes a bundle of imposing probabilities, some of which are very near to being proven.' He complained that religion was being confused with science, 'with the result that feelings have run high and reason has been led astray. If, instead of Christ, there were a question of someone like a Sargon, an Achilles or one of the Pharaohs, no one would have thought of making any objection.'

By the time Vignon's book came out, however, the critics had found their second wind. The reviewer in *Nature* wrote, 'Dr Vignon is either the victim of credulity or he has overdone his evidence to such an extent as to have damaged his own reputation as a scientific witness ... it reads like an antiquarian dissertation ending in a pseudo-scientific anti-climax.' The writer had already stated his conviction that whether this was or was not the Shroud of Christ 'is a question which need not be seriously considered in the columns of a scientific publication'; it was, therefore, clearly always beyond Vignon's power to gain his approbation when dealing with that question above all.

Now, for a long time, the waves of history simply closed over Vignon's book. It was as though he had not worked at all. The sceptics, basing themselves either on scientific puritanism or historical orthodoxy (the first ignoring the question and the second taking its answer from the Bishop of Troyes) held the field. In Britain, the careful denunciations of Father Herbert Thurston, a Jesuit polemicist of wide scholarship and subtle argument, quieted even the faithful; non-believers had, of course, no reason to reopen the issue. Yet Thurston's view that the Shroud image was a painting modified by the action of time matched neither scientific fact nor theologian's logic. As an eventual opponent, the Irish priest, Father Beecher, pointed out, this was a theory that demanded skill in a painter unheard of in the Late Middle Ages and met with very rarely since, as well as pigments, whether water or oil based, that had at the time in question only a notional existence. Such fourteenth-century pigments as were known were all discounted by Vignon's objections. And Vignon's counter to the view that an artist had been responsible still held good: how had the picture with all its detail been reversed from positive to negative? And if it had been painted in the negative, why and for whom, five centuries before photography? It was a case of the blind painting for the blind.

In May, 1931, the Shroud was once more placed on public exhibition in Turin. It was then that Giuseppi Enrie took his careful and now-famous pictures. As these were printed, it at once became clear that detail much finer than anything visible in Pia's photographs was revealed by them. As a result, in enlargement they finally resolved beyond argument the pigment question: each thread of the material could be distinctly seen and no clogging was visible in the spaces in between. It was inconceivable that any pigment able to survive over the centuries should not have clung to every part and level of the fabric.

It was from these prints, too, that experts were able to make some assessment of the weave. Its herringbone pattern proved to be one known in Asiatic linens not only of that period but even before. In Europe, however, it was not woven until the fourteenth century was long over. There was no objection here, therefore, to the gathering conviction that this was indeed the Shroud in which Jesus had lain in the hours before his resurrection.

The interest aroused by the Shroud's exhibition and the Enrie photographs resulted in a second wave of scientific investigation. One whose work was to prove a comprehensive breaker all on its own was Pierre Bartet, another French polymath, a linguist and sensitive translator of poetry, a gifted amateur violinist, a sportsman proficient in tennis, swimming and riding, but by profession a successful surgeon and teacher of anatomy. It is arguable whether in his work on the Shroud it was an advantage or a drawback that he was also an intense and devout Christian.

He began his investigation by considering the nature of the wounds displayed by the man on the Shroud. A meticulous man, he decided to test whether a nail could actually pass through the wrist at the point indicated by the image. Visualising the structure of bone, nerve and sinew that lay beneath the skin, he rather doubted the possibility. He made the necessary test by the simplest method possible: taking an arm he had himself amputed only a little while before, he drove a nail through the wrist as near to the precise point displayed on the Shroud as he could. To his surprise, despite some difficulty and resistance, the nail thrust through in exactly that place. Much greater surprise, though, was caused by the reaction of the thumb, which had jerked back to lie flat along the palm.

Sceptics had always seized on the fact that the Shroud image showed no thumbs. If it was indeed a direct impression of a man, this seemed a peculiar oversight on the part of whatever process had caused it. Now perhaps Barbet had discovered the explanation. When he examined the wrist in detail, he found that the powerful drive of the nail through the flesh had caused great damage to the median nerve. The muscles in the hand that it controlled had responded by flexing automatically and, as a result, had pulled the thumb flat against the palm. This happened on each of the several occasions when Barbet repeated this rather gruesome experiment. As had happened so often in Shroud experimentation, what at first had appeared a valid criticism had been reversed to become evidence for authenticity. No fourteenth-century forger, surely, could have known a fact only made plain by the experimentation of a twentieth-century surgeon.

Barbet now became curious about the fact that two runnels of blood, rather than one, flowed along the arm from the wrist wounds, at different angles. Assuming the constancy of gravity, the likeliest cause was that during the crucifixion the arms had been maintained in two alternate positions. This would have been possible only if the whole body, too, had shifted between two alternate attitudes. When Barbet began to study the matter in greater detail, he discovered that if the whole weight of the body had been taken on the crucified, spread-eagled arms, the victim would have died very swiftly from suffocation. It was for that reason that the feet were also nailed to the cross. They took some of the weight, preventing that pulling down and constriction of the rib-cage which would have brought an earlier release.

There was thus a constant shifting in the position of the crucified: he would slump down, his weight on the nails in his wrist. Soon the pressure across his chest and the restriction on his breathing would force him forward and up, putting his weight now on the nail through his feet. After a while the agony this caused would force him to drop again. So it would go, hour after hour, the slow, agonised rise, the appalling collapse, an endless slow-motion fluttering, as though he were some pinned bird nailed down by the inexorable hunters of the world: and so perhaps he was. Barbet, being a scientist, naturally quantified his findings. In the first position, with the weight on the wrists, the arms made an angle of 65° with the vertical; in the second, the angle was some five degrees greater. The doctor made some tests that confirmed that when the arms were pinned level with the shoulders and the body drooped between them, its lowest possible position would, in fact, drag down the arms to the 65° angle he had deduced from the blood flow.

In 1933, Barbet travelled to Turin to see the Shroud during its exhibition that year. He wanted to look at its actual colours. When he did, however, he was seized with an overwhelming awe. With a sense of wonder so dazzling that it brought him instantly to his knees, he realised that the stains he had been so energetically and objectively analysing from the photographs had truly been made by blood. A surgeon, he said, could recognise that immediately and without the slightest doubt. With absolute conviction he claimed that what he had seen was 'the blood that had sunk into the linen, and this blood was the Blood of Christ!"

Back in Paris and restored to scientific objectivity, Barbet began a new series of experiments. One set was concerned with establishing, as he had with the wrists, the precise position of the nail that had pierced the feet. The Shroud depicted the feet as having been crossed with the left above the right and then fixed to the cross by a single nail. Again working with actual specimens, Barbet showed that it was between and above the second and third toes that the spike had been driven. More complicated, and perhaps more interesting, was the work he did on the wound in the figure's side. 'But when they came to Jesus, and saw that he was dead already, they brake not his legs: But one of the soldiers with a spear pierced his side, and forthwith came there out blood and water.' So had run St John's description of the moment when that wound was made; now Barbet had the evidence of it before him. It had always seemed like one strand in the gigantic miracle of that sacrifice – the man already dead, the spear plunged in, the sudden rush of blood and fluid from a body where all should long before have been congealed ...

Barbet first of all placed, by precise measurement, where exactly the wound lay; it was between the fifth and sixth ribs. He knew, and proved again on the bodies that lay on his dissecting table, that in the right auricle of a dead man's heart there was a reservoir of blood which did not clot or harden for a considerable period. That right auricle lay not more than four inches from where the wound had gaped. It would certainly account for the blood. But the water?

Barbet now took a hollow needle attached to an empty syringe. Very slowly he inserted it into the side of a cadaver. The moment he felt the tip pierce the outer membrane of the heart, he stopped his controlled thrust and squeezed the bulb of the syringe. A colourless fluid surged up the narrow tube – the pericardial fluid. The outermost covering of the heart is called the pericardial sac; and this serum is called hydropericardium. He pushed further, squeezed again; this time it was blood that came rushing up the tube. As in the Bible, he had brought 'blood and water' to well out of a corpse. He, however, had been very careful; the soldier had struck a violent blow. Would that have had the same effect? Barbet gathered himself, raised his arm, then struck with a surgeon's precision. Almost at once, blood began to pour from the wound he had made – and with it came a clear liquid: hydropericardium.

His concentration on the wounds of the Shroud image constantly confronted the devout – perhaps over-devout – Barbet with the reality of Christ's sufferings. He brooded over them; he had them constantly in mind. Step by step and over and over again, he seemed to move with Jesus through His inexorable agony. He wrote about that agony in 'The Corporal Passion of Jesus Christ', included in the book he published; its English title was *Doctor at Calvary*, suggesting that he was a direct witness to that death or perhaps even a participant in the events that surrounded it. The vividness with which his trained yet over-imaginative eye set these scenes before him almost broke his health and undermined his reason. Eventually he had to turn away, as though from some great light too strong for his vision. 'I can assure you of a dreadful thing', he wrote, 'I have reached the point when I no longer dare to think of them. No doubt this is cowardice, but I hold ... that one must be either a saint or else irresponsible in order to do the Way of the Cross. I no longer can.'

Paul Vignon, meanwhile, as he moved into old age, had not lost his interest in the Holy Shroud. Over the years, his book, at least in France, had gained an honourable reputation as a fascinating attempt – if not more – to unravel the truth or falsehood of the relic. He now shifted his ground from that of scientist to that of historian, proposing in the late thirties a precursor of the theory today propounded by Ian Wilson. He suggested that the remarkably homogeneous view of Jesus that prevailed among artists from the fifth century onwards derived, in fact, from the Shroud. It was that image which had served as model for all later depictions. One of the examples he cited as probably based on the Shroud was the Image of Edessa.

Of course Vignon had no proof to offer for this theory; he merely used it to counter the scepticism about the close resemblance between the Shroud image and the most widely accepted artists' versions of Jesus. It was typical of the fertility and originality of his mind that he should have taken that criticism and reversed it: far from the figure on the Shroud conforming to some prevailing idea, he suggested, the prevailing idea conformed to the figure on the Shroud. It made sense to propose that the similarity in the many depictions of Jesus had its origins in one reliable model, and what model could be more reliable than the actual presentation of the face and body of Jesus, preserved since the moment of His tormented death? The difficulty was that no one had ever stated that the Shroud had served in this capacity. Wilson, of course, avoids this problem by proposing that the Shroud and the Image of Edessa are one and the same. It follows that no one could have claimed that the Shroud was, as it were, the basic icon of Christianity – they were not even aware of the Shroud's existence. It is Wilson's thesis that the Shroud, durings its travels in Asia Minor and Byzantium, was folded into four and framed, like a portrait. He cites some evidence to support this idea, and if it is accepted then the Shroud during those centuries was 'hidden' while in full view of the world, a little like the envelope on the correspondence rack in *The Purloined Letter*.

Paul Vignon died in 1943, his country under Nazi domination, his health overwhelmed by cancer; to his final moment he was watched from above his bed by the powerful yet dolorous face he had come firmly to believe was that of Jesus Christ. Shroud studies, of course, continued. Conferences – notably in 1939 and 1950 – took further, where they could, the work of the early pioneers. In 1969 and 1973, as has been said, the authorities of Turin Cathedral under Cardinal Pellegrino themselves gathered a commission of enquiry to take a deeper scientific look at the cloth. All the work that was done continued to produce corroborative results. For example, the extreme concavity of the abdomen displayed by the Shroud image was shown to be yet another physical consequence of crucifixion. The blood flow on the side of the body conforms to the contours of the ribcage, validating the basis of Barbet's work with the blood flows on the arms. Small advances, perhaps, no more than ancillary investigations, but each had its importance.

The results of the Turin enquiry were perhaps a little disappointing. There were those who thought the investigating scientists might have been, on the whole, a little more distinguished and drawn from somewhat further afield. Shroud studies were in a state of rapid development, a rapidity that matched the progress in the technology of scientific research generally. Any commission gathered to investigate an object of such consuming interest ought to have reflected the best talents active anywhere in the world, and in all the relevant specialities. Instead, those who met in Turin Cathedral included three priests, the representative of ex-King Umberto – the head of the house of Savoy is still the Shroud's nominal owner – and a gaggle of North Italian academics. Although these were on the whole both proficient and objective, their local origins made it seem as though the Cathedral authorities wanted in some way to keep close control of a more or less parochial investigation. This may be an unfair impression, but the arrangements fell far short of permitting the world scientific community access to the Shroud. What reinforced these doubts was the fact that for over three years the names of those on the commission were actually kept secret.

In one important respect, however, the 1973

investigations demonstrated a new liberalism on the part of the authorities. All the extraordinarily detailed work that had been done on the Shroud since 1900 had had to rely on photographs. Now, for the first time, scientists were not only allowed to examine it at some leisure, but even to remove samples of its very fibre. Indeed, the preliminary meeting four years earlier had already listed precisely what samples would be required. This was the moment when Shroud investigations began their most recent and most intense phase, a phase made possible by ecclesiastical co-operation and given added vigour and a precise focus by the needs of David Rolfe's *The Silent Witness*.

CHAPTER FOUR

With the fundamental problem of finance solved, all the normal difficulties that rear up during the production of a film had to be faced. David Rolfe now had to bring together the necessary team, decide where and what they should film, liaise with the countries to which the story of the Shroud would lead them, and make sure that there was a shooting script upon which they could base their work.

All this created a completely different set of what may be called political circumstances from those which had surrounded his attempts to fund the film. First, David had to allay the doubts of Ian Wilson, who at times felt that his project was being hijacked. His original script, as was only natural, had expounded his own views. Now, as the scope of the film widened and its research horizons receded, more and more people, and therefore more and more ideas, had to be accommodated. The leaders of the Holy Shroud Guild in America, who had after all been deeply instrumental in finding the essential finance, felt themselves entitled to have some say in the project. So did Harry John. So, most emphatically, did David Rolfe. He wanted his film to include all the relevant work being done around the world; it was for that reason that he had already tried to contact the people in Colorado and Arizona who, as Father Rinaldi had told him, were conducting their own experiments on the Shroud image. He also wanted it to be a good film; exposition by itself would not hold the interest of audiences. He proposed adding a screenwriter to his team, a decision with which Wilson was not entirely happy. For the first time, a measure of friction became apparent between the two men.

It was not only the internal politics of his film-making team, however, that David had to face. The Shroud was, in one sense, the property of the world. In another, it belonged to the Catholic Church. The Vatican expert on it was Monsignor Giulio Ricci. His ideas about the Shroud and its image were, in many particulars, unique to him. He had published them, he lectured on them, he ran classes in Shroud studies from a well-appointed centre in Rome established for that purpose. He felt to an alarming degree proprietorial about the Shroud. He could not be excluded from the film, if only because Harry John knew and valued him. If he were included, however, his pietistic assumptions about the identity of the image, his certainty that it proved not only the truth of the crucifixion but also that Jesus had died overcome with love for sinful, suffering mankind, threatened to upset the clarity and objectivity upon which David had insisted from the beginning. Monsignor Ricci represented a force, intellectual as well as theological, which David would have to compromise with, circumvent or overcome.

The first stage, however, was to sort out the places where the Shroud may have been, where he and his unit would have to film. He organised a journey of reconnaissance for Wilson and himself, taking Max Frei, too, in fulfilment of the obligation he had undertaken to the Swiss criminologist. In November, 1976, he and Wilson flew to Istanbul, to rendezvous with Dr Frei at the Intercontinental Hotel.

David had been in the Middle East, working on films in Dhubai and Kuweit on the Persian Gulf, and inland in the Arabian peninsula, but had never visited Turkey. The ramshackle mixture of the traditional old and the enforced and hectic new, of Asia and Europe, East and West, seemed to him both exciting and distasteful. Yet there could be no doubts about the beauty and interest of the ancient buildings that figured in the history of the Shroud.

Standing under the scarred, unsteady walls that are all that remain of the Church of the Virgin Mary at

Blachernae, he tried to visualise its long-departed glories. It was here that for centuries Byzantium's most precious relic, the Robe of the Virgin, had been kept, its cloth, so emperors and citizens fervently believed, imbued with the power to defeat invaders. Just over a thousand years before, the Image of Edessa had been carried in ceremonial triumph into this church, to remain for a little while beside the Robe. For the people of Byzantium, it was as though Mother and Son had been reunited within their city walls.

After a short stay, the Mandylion had travelled by galley, like an honoured visitor, up the Bosphorus to the Golden Horn. Above the sluggish, slapping waves of that fabled waterway, as though suspended between the continents, David and his companions were one evening to eat, in a restaurant built out above the water. Perhaps on that occasion in 944 the Byzantines had done the same, devouring, then as now, their skewered meat, poultry, rice or pulses, and dark red wines. The next day, however, they would have clustered into the streets or clambered on to their battlements in order to see the portrait of Jesus carried in its casket to the Golden Gate and so at evening, into the city, amid the wild resonance of music and the crimson glare of innumerable torches.

It was in what remained of that cluttered, hysterical, gold-encrusted city that Max Frei now began his investigations. On the walls of the ancient churches and palaces, pitted by time, grew many different varieties of plants. Dr Frei collected these, plucking specimens to dry, placing them in his special boxes and envelopes, hoping eventually to match their pollens to those, still unidentified, which he had taken from the Shroud. David, meanwhile, immersed himself in the atmosphere of the country and the city. He watched the hundreds of boats that ferried thousands upon thousands of patient men and women to and from the European shore every morning and night. It was entrancing, magical, a glimpse into some mythological dimension, the boats dark against the bright water, the people vociferous here, there subdued, the craft crowding against each other, some so well designed for their cramped work that they seemed able to manoeuvre sideways.

He had also heard through film editor, Tom Priestly (the son of J.B. Priestly, the writer) of a man who might act as his location manager in Turkey. His name was Samin Deger, and he proved to be not only a stocky, square-faced man of integrity and great charm but intelligent, articulate and endlessly resourceful into the bargain. 'He was marvellous', David says. 'Absolutely brilliant!' In time, he was to prove it, and not only by introducing his companions to that romantic – if somewhat unsteady – restaurant built out over the oily Bosphorus.

With Istanbul firmly established in their minds and Dr Frei's investigations completed, it was time to move further east, to Urfa, the ancient Edessa. David had booked flights to Diyabakir in London but learned in Istanbul that Urfa's airport had been closed. He tried to work out an alternative route with the aid of the official Tourist Office, a venture which appeared slightly less than promising from the moment when the clerk on duty had difficulties in finding Urfa on the map. Eventually, it was decided that they should fly to the east coast town of Adana. There, they were assured, they would find a taxi to drive them the remaining five hundred kilometers or so to their destination.

They flew to Adana where spirited bargaining obtained for them their promised taxi ride. With feelings of optimism and adventure that they set off toward Gaziente and Urfa. The road wound up through pleasant hills and down along fertile valleys with green trees, olive groves and signs of cultivation. Beyond Gaziente, however, as the plain began to stretch out in every direction, the aspect changed; the harvest was over and to the uninstructed eye all was desolation. Later journeys revealed the inaccuracy of this impression, but this first time the endless levels of brown and dun and pale orange stretched away to featureless horizons. Depression settled about them like the seeping dust that fell endlessly out of the wind. They felt that they had entered a desert.

Then they began to notice the accidents. Averaging one every twenty-five kilometers, these punctuated with their gruesome witness the monotony of their progress. In one, a car had evidently, only moments before, smashed into a small truck and a Citroen before careering over the edge of a low cliff. Blood and entrails lay across the road, a sinister trail worse than the evidence of other disasters only because so recently laid down.

As the kilometers trickled by the taxi driver began to show signs of distress. He was, he explained, in pain. His abdomen, his stomach ... It was hard for him to be precise. But there was strong and increasing discomfort; he might have to stop or he might have to turn round and go back. To David it seemed strange that he, unused to Turkish food, should feel so well when this stout native of the country was clearly suffering. The taxi stopped in a small town. With a final groan the man got out; a moment later he was negotiating with a local driver. There were nods, agreements. He came back. He had to return home, he said; he could not continue – but had made for them adequate alternative arrangements. Thus, as they bumped their way towards Urfa, they were accompanied in their new taxi by a round, taciturn lady and a ruffled hen. It was only later that David discovered the reason for their first driver's mysterious illness – in England that evening Liverpool were playing a European Cup match against the Turkish side Trabzon! Unhappily, David recalled that, in his sympathy for the man's sudden illness, he had agreed to pay him the full fare.

It was later that night that David really became aware of that televised match – one of Urfa's few sets stood outside his hotel room and drew a large and vociferous congregation of supporters. Kick-off was at two, local time, in the morning! For what seemed like the rest of the night the amplified voice of the commentator, the roars of both the distant crowd and the present viewers and the criticisms of over-heated hecklers resounded through the vast marble-walled lobby. This was the one gesture towards grandeur in a building otherwise progressing towards decrepitude. (It was on his second visit that David discovered its only WC, hidden behind a door, the key to which had to be procured on each necessary occasion by special application to the management.) The rooms were dirty, with beds in every available space – that David, Wilson and Max Frei each wanted a separate, single room was almost beyond the desk-clerk's comprehension. The atmosphere seemed initially so depressing that one night two American ladies wept on each other's shoulder at the prospect of having to sleep there. Yet, such is the triumph of humanity over circumstance, David now remembers this hostelry with nostalgia, for the people who work there came, in his three visits, to know him and he regards them as something akin to friends. They were helpful, energetic, happy to do what they could for his comfort and, later, that of his film crew. In memory, the building dims; those who people it become clearer.

They had arrived in Urfa as night was falling so it was not until the next morning that they had their first clear look at the town. It lies between belts of low limestone hills; on one bluff rise the shattered columns of a Roman citadel, lonely markers to a vanished glory. In the centuries before Christ, Urfa had been a place of some importance, controlling as it did one of the passes that led to the lush riches of Mesopotamia. It was probably at least four thousand years old, for in the fourteenth century BC a Hittite army had destroyed it, and there was a tradition going back much further which claimed it as the birthplace of Abraham. In the citadel-hill is a cave that locals point out to visitors as the very spot where the patriarch was born.

There clearly is some connection, at least in legend, between Abraham and Urfa – if not the city, then the region. Genesis relates how Abraham and his people took 'all their substance that they had gathered, and the souls that they had gotten in Haran; and they went forth to go into the land of Canaan; and into the land of Canaan they came'. It was the continuation of a journey that had begun with their departure from Ur of the Chaldees. The family had stopped in Haran perhaps because Teräh, Abraham's father, had died there. The town of Harran stands on Turkey's border with Syria, some thirty miles from Urfa, and has been identified as the settlement mentioned in Genesis. It may be, that in myth or truth the man whom both Jews and Arabs consider their progenitor had passed through the town.

It was for this reason that Urfa's principal attraction for the tourist was the famous Fish Ponds of Abraham. These were sacred pools, fed by a deep, clear spring, which had existed there for many centuries – no one knows how many. The waters of these ponds are constantly stirred by a vast colony of fish, a seething population of carp or trout which no one is permitted to catch. Swimming round and round their ornamental pools, in a public garden dominated by the slim minaret of a nearby religious school, the fish lead lives of enviable luxury, of absolute security. At the waterside peddlers make a living by selling little bags of nuts and seeds to visitors with which to feed them.

The origin of these small lakes, and of their name, lies beyond history. The legend David heard links Abraham with Nimrod, the 'mighty hunter' of the Bible who was probably the Assyrian Ninurta, god of war and of hunting. He has connections, too, with the Sumerian fire-god, Nusku – and this leads back to the story, for Nimrod is supposed to have flung Abraham on fire from the skies to the earth. But the flames of the fire turned to water and the wood that fed them became fish; doused, the patriarch survived. The ponds and their occupants have been sacred ever since. Today, in a small boat, one may paddle across them, seeing at dusk the reflections of dozens of little coloured lights, a shifting brightness lifting off the tiny waves. As in so many places in the Middle East, present is linked through millenia to the past by the stones and streams amongst which one moves. Every cave and building, every stream and tree, every mark in the landscape, hints at history, myth and the watchful interventions of the divine.

Urfa is not only famous in the history of religion because of the Image of Edessa but also because it was perhaps the first Christian settlement in Asia Minor, one of the first known anywhere. Its beliefs were, of course, those still propagated by the Nestorians – most of whom, the surviving rump of a once great sect within the Eastern Church, now live and worship in San Francisco. A Patriarch of Constantinople, Nestorius preached that the divine in Christ's nature was not derived from his human heritage. Mary was the mother of Jesus, not the Mother of God. The consequent demotion of the Virgin and, more important theologically, the increased importance this gave to the human nature of Christ, caused violent and acrimonious dissension in the early Church. Nestorius proved the loser. In 435 he was exiled to the desert, living out his remaining years in the featureless Egyptian sands. But his teachings survived – and their centre of propagation, for another half-century, was the Christian School of Edessa. Perhaps because the town lay athwart the principal trade route to the East, Nestorian beliefs spread in that direction. By the seventh century, and probably much earlier, Nestorian missionaries had penetrated as far as China. By then, of course, Edessa was safely within the patriarchal jurisdiction of an established Orthodoxy, and the centre of Nestorian activity had shifted to Persia. A thousand years after heresy had first animated the breasts of Edessa's theologians, the city fell to the Turks and its part in the Christian story ended.

Its position on a vital road ensured its importance as a market town. David, though interested in the citadel, in the sacred fish, in the ruined castle that overlooks the town from the west, found himself much more fascinated by the brilliance, the scents, the cries and gesticulations, the patience, poverty and triumphs of the market. Peasants watchful behind their produce, dark Arabs, camel-borne from Syria, immobile goatherds surrounded by their flocks like monarchs at court, beaters of copper cheek-by-jowl with sellers of plastic cups, and these beside the dusty booths where, with a rhythmic stamping and a steady kicking, carpets of felt were being rolled and pounded, rolled and pounded on the bare stone floor. Wherever he looked movement and colour would resolve itself into a sharply-etched scene as absorbing as a fairytale.

Meanwhile, Dr Frei ranged the surrounding escarpments, happily collecting the specimens that would fill out his chapter in the story of the Shroud. Just as importantly, he met and made friends with the director of the local metereological station. As a result he was able to obtain crucial information on such seasonal factors as the prevailing winds, the fluctuating effects of the seasons and so on. As for Ian Wilson, he seemed to have come home. David found it almost impossible to believe that for him, too, this was a first visit to Urfa. He picked his way among the city's monuments as though a lifetime's experience had trained him as a guide. So steeped had he become, over the last fifteen years, in the history of the place, its antiquities seemed now no more than the physical manifestations of something he had always known. These were the stones which – although he had never seen them – he had been living with for years.

Wilson's most interesting finding about Urfa, however, occurred after they had already long left the city. They were actually flying home when, browsing through the photographs they had collected, he let out a sudden yell: 'Look!' David leaned over. Wilson pointed to an aerial view of gardens and water.

'Can you see an outline there?'

And, yes, David could – a faint ghost of something perhaps a building, which had left an indentation, a mere suggestion of an outline, stretching across the bare, stone-dappled ground, the scrubby shruds and mean, gnawed grass.

'Yes', he said. 'Yes – a sort of ... Certainly a shape. What is it?'

Wilson frowned. 'I'll tell you what I think it is. Justinian built a cathedral in Edessa. It was as big as Saint Sophia in Byzantium itself. It's vanished, destroyed centuries ago: there were so many Muslim invaders ... No one's ever been able to find the site. I think this is it.'

If Wilson is right, the building must have been vast. The outline on the picture would appear to be the apse. It faces east. In the street beyond, a few trucks, quite dwarfed, give an idea of its scale. Expert archaeologists think the suggestion that it really is Edessa's Saint Sophia, found at last, is more than plausible. Will anyone ever investigate further? Certainly not in the immediate future – perhaps never, given the continuing anti-Christian bias still to be found in Turkey. And then, in the Middle East – as in Urfa itself, with its castle and its citadel – there are so many potential sites, thousands upon thousands, that no one but, perhaps, the occasional thief or grave robber has ever investigated. A century from now, the curious and the interested will doubtless be able to deplore as energetically as we do now how small a part of that huge archaeological task has ever been attempted.

After Turkey came the other stage of their reconnaissance – Israel. At Tel Aviv, the airport authorities singled David out for extended questioning, perhaps because of the many Arabian stamps in his passport. Then came another long taxi-ride through a pale-brown, grey and yellow landscape. Agriculture interposed its various greens and there was scrub on the dusty hills. Here and there a burned-out tank or truck reminded one of the country's beleaguered situation. Among the peeling façades of noisy Arab towns they were to see the sullen faces of a people under occupation, evidence of a resentment, unsoftened by the manifest prosperity, which at intervals broke out into terrorism. The divisions in the Middle East, the vestiges of war which were their legacy, the frequent sight of men under arms, all helped to give to their visit a deep-seated feeling of anxiety, hidden as well as they could.

Nothing, however, could dim David's excitement at seeing from a distance, then at being in, the city of Jerusalem. He believed the Shroud to be authentic. It was here, therefore, that it had originated, here that it had been used. He wandered through narrow streets, watching the endless rapid bowing of Jews at prayer beside the Wailing Wall and seeking evidence of Jesus's crucifixion and death.

These, to a certain extent, disappointed him. The Church of the Holy Sepulchre was, after all, just another vast, over-decorated building. More to his taste was the little garden beside the tomb unearthed by General Gordon. It was tranquil, full of the gentle delights that plants offer. Unfortunately, he had with him his expert. Max Frei was quite categorical – not one of the flowers in that garden was indigenous to the country. Not one could have grown there two thousand years ago. They had all been introduced by eager Protestants over-anxious to make beautiful the surroundings of 'their' tomb, the post-Reformation riposte to the Catholic assertion of that grandiose church.

As he travelled, David began to see the stories of the Bible framed by the physical structures of the country. It was a frame that seemed to give them both a new validity and a new urgency. More than that, they took on a human dimension which, while not diminishing them in the slightest, robbed them of their cold, mythological distance and brought them within reach. He stared out across the Sea of Galilee and thought to himself, 'Why, it's no larger than Lake Windermere!' He could imagine now the gatherings at the lake, the people clustering around their Teacher, while even from the far shore men, made curious by a crowd which they could see so easily, clambered into their boats in order to take part in the event. In a place like that, word of a new kind of preaching would spread in days, and every phrase and nuance offered by the preacher would be almost instantaneously taken up that eager public.

David floated in the Dead Sea, made uneasy by its unnatural buoyancy and sick by its salts when, trying to swim, he swallowed a mouthful of water. He travelled to the Lebanese border to climb the heights of Massada. There, he stared out across the brown plain in the warm breeze that had once touched Herod's hair and tried to imagine the besieging Roman legions down below. Patient and disciplined in the heat, they had waited for two bitter years while, high above them, the Jewish rebels' reserves of water and strength ran out. Only courage had remained to them in the end – and death, as one by one they had turned to suicide rather than surrender. They had left behind the signs of their resistance, a token to the Israelis of a later day who made their pilgrimage up that cliff-face in order to reaffirm their own faith and shore up their own courage. David watched them, and Jews from all over the world, and tourists who were not Jews, journey up to the narrow plateau, stage for that distant drama; some disdained the cable car that might have taken them in relative comfort to the top, scrambling along the paths that wound up the cliff face as though to prove their own hardihood and valour. A few of these did indeed carry on until they dropped, almost fainting in the heavy November heat.

Israel, with its holy places and ancient towns – Bethlehem, Nazareth – making palpable the existence of Jesus, making it less and less possible to doubt His historical reality, had a profound effect on David as a man. As a film producer, however, he was less enthusiastic about it. It was a very expensive country; the story of the Shroud, rather than the events that had apparently created it, was his main concern – and that had largely occurred elsewhere; as a location, the Church of the Holy

Sepulchre seemed to him at once too well known and too vulgar, while the Garden Tomb had to be discounted because of Dr Frei's expert testimony. For all these reasons, there seemed little reason to film in the Holy Land itself, when such scenes as he needed could without difficulty be reproduced elsewhere.

Even the researches of Max Frei could be duplicated for the film. The wilderness of Judaea, where the Swiss scientist had been collecting his plants, looked little different from the landscapes to be found near Urfa. The relevant sequence in the film could easily be shot there. As a result David, although he did make some tentative contacts with Israeli film-makers, had more or less determined before he left the country that he would not be returning there with a camera crew. The only person who might be sorry was Max Frei. Not having been to Israel before, he revelled in this new playground. Once he had discovered two or three varieties relevant to the film's purposes, however, his work would hardly need to be repeated in any detail. Satisfied with the work that had been done, David prepared for the journey home.

The exigencies of Arab-Israeli acrimony produced one more odd twist in the tale of his Middle Eastern experiences, however. At Tel Aviv airport, where on arrival he had been put through so stringent an interrogation, he was again taken out of the line of waiting passengers. In a quiet office he found himself facing a cool, dark-haired man in his early thirties who seemed, despite superficial politenesses, to be appraising him with the hard eyes of a jewel thief examining a tiara. He was, he told David, the head of the airport security system. He said, "I wonder, Mr Rolfe, if you'd do us a favour?"

Surprised, David asked what it was. The man smiled. 'You'll realise that we have the constant problem here of keeping our officers on their toes. In order to make sure that they are, we arrange occasional dummy runs by people we know but they don't. We'd like you to be one of them.'

David stared at him. 'Make a dummy run for you? Go through the security checks?'

'That's right.'

'Will I actually be carrying something?'

From a drawer the man brought out a small automatic. The blue steel of the short barrel had a smooth, sinister sheen. He held it up, his finger curled round the trigger guard. Both he and David looked at it. David shrugged.

'Won't it be dangerous? They might decide to shoot me.'

'We provide you with special papers', the man said, reassuringly, then waited. David considered the risks, balancing them against the attractions of adventure. He smiled, nodded. 'All right', he said. 'I'll have a go at it.'

It was with some tension, therefore, that he approached the baggage search. In the little cubicle, the officer, neat and precise, took his hand luggage. As though mesmerised, David watched him open it. The gun was packed with a bundle of soiled clothes in a small plastic bag. Deftly, the searching hands separated the contents of the case. Books, paper handkerchiefs, wash-bag; then the laundry, brought out, laid to one side. A comb, chocolates, a small carved wooden camel for his daughter ... Satisfied, the man began to repack the case. He lifted the laundry, about to put it back, and then stopped. For a second, looking down, his expression preoccupied, he seemed to be weighing it in his hand. His other hand reached in. The next moment he was in violent motion.

David was flung against the wall of the cubicle. The man's elbow was in his throat, strangling him. The weight of his body, pinning David, prevented him from moving; with his free hand he pressed a bell. At the same time he was yelling, ferociously repeating a number. The door burst open. A soldier stood on the threshold, sub-machine-gun thrust forward. For a second, David thought he was about to be killed. Then, over the soldier's shoulder, he saw the calm, dark face of the Director of Security.

'OK. Relax. One of ours.' Slowly the soldier lowered his gun. The officer moved away, backing off like a cat that may yet decide to spring. He took a deep breath, looking from David to the Director. For his part, David was bent forward, gasping, feeling now as though he had just done three rounds in a wrestling ring. The Director smiled.

He said to David, 'Of course, sometimes they shoot first ... After all, we've had so much trouble here. But thank you. Thank you very much. It was very kind of you to help us. Very sporting.'

Later David asked the officer who had searched his luggage what would have happened if he had, in fact, been able to carry the hand-gun through to his plane. The man shrugged, 'The moment you took off I'd have been walking up that road without a job. What do you think? We don't get second chances in this business. You make a mistake and you're sacked. Or dead.'

In this melodramatic fashion David made his exit from Israel. Overall, he was pleased with the results of his journey. Istanbul, Urfa, Jerusalem, all were now real places in his mind. He could plan around them. He had local knowledge. More than that, he had useful contacts there, agents who could act for him. He had fulfilled his obligation to Dr Frei and would soon receive in return the criminologist's definitive report. It was already clear that the field-trip had extended the favourable nature of Max Frei's evidence. Back in London, it was with some optimism that he sat down to draft his first report to Harry John's de Rance Foundation, to Father Otterbein and to Father Rinaldi of the Holy Shroud Guild.

Briefly, he dealt with the days they had spent in Istanbul. He envisaged 'practical problems' while filming in Turkey, but to help deal with these he had been, he wrote, 'fortunate in obtaining the services of a Turkish film-maker and production manager, Samin Deger, who ... will coordinate both technical requirements and the various official requirements for filming both in Istanbul and Urfa.'

His visit to the latter city he described as 'without doubt the most fascinating part of the trip. It is relatively undeveloped and has few facilities for visitors. The few hotels are primitive by any standards'. The language of official reports can hardly go further. The town itself, he added, 'abounds in arçhaeological treasures, mostly unappreciated and, in some cases, actually abused by the inhabitants. Judging from photographs taken six years ago, even within such a short time several historical sites and objects have been defaced, either wilfully or by lack of care ... Parts of the West Gate of the city, in which the Shroud was hidden as a result of the persecution, still remain, although this is one of the relics that is deteriorating quickly through inadequate protection'. Mentioning both the discovery of the lost Cathedral – 'amazing and fortunate', he felt – and the continuing work of Dr Frei, he then passed on to the Israeli part of the trip.

Jerusalem had, he wrote, 'surprisingly little of direct relevance to the film. Those locations that can be connected with the Shroud, particularly the site of the tomb, have been gradually developed and enshrined so that the actual features have been lost to view ... Another significant location visited was Acre, the treasury of the highly secretive and powerful order of the Knights Templar and which would have been the temporary resting place of the Shroud after its theft from Constantinople and its subsequent journey to Europe. The Crusader influence on the city is still very evident ...'

'It was a very encouraging and, in many ways, exciting trip.' His one-sentence summing up was a measure of his gathering optimism. It was with brisk confidence that he watched the turning of the year. But 1977, he knew, would see his venture either made – or broken.

CHAPTER FIVE

One direct consequence of the journey to the Middle East was that Dr Frei was at last able to finish his report on the origins of the pollens he had found. He named five plants from the desert regions of the Holy Land, two which grew habitually on the desert borders. Two of the pollens derived from plants that grew in Turkey. In addition, there were spores from at least eight other Mediterranean plants.

This enabled Max Frei to be much more categorical than before. He wrote, 'Apart from what we already know from historical sources about the displays at Torino, Vercelli and Chambéry, which have left their traces, it is possible in the actual state of our knowledge to confirm that the Shroud is contaminated with pollen from desert plants growing in Israel, from a forest plant and a species from the steppe of Turkey, and from a grass from the sand-dunes of the Mediterranean shores. The greatest number of pollen grains identified comes from Mediterranean plants which grow in Palestine, at Istanbul and partly at Torino.'

There was thus no question of the scientific evidence undermining Ian Wilson's original theory. Instead, it had been supported: the Shroud had apparently been in the places Wilson said it had. This did not, of course, make his ideas true – there was probably no proof imaginable upon which one could base historical connections of the sort he was proposing – but it confirmed that they had to be taken seriously. The idea that the Shroud had existed in Asia Minor long enough to pick up the pollen spores but without attracting attention, seemed ridiculous, especially when one remembered the Byzantine addiction to relics. If one conceded, therefore, that it had been known, one had to add that it could not have been known by its present description. Of something as precious as the Shroud of Christ we would have had news, just as we have had news of the putative Robe of the Virgin. If it was known, under yet another name, how many such objects were available? A tiny cluster of miraculous portraits, the age of most of which have been proved not to be of great antiquity. With the evidence of Max Frei, Wilson's arguments took on a new strength. David might have been anxious over the possibility that Frei's first field-trip would undermine the whole venture, that the closer look would have negated the encouraging results of his laboratory examination. As it was, he could relax; he was still very much on course.

Early morning in the Chapel of the Shroud, 16 June, 1969. It was here that the Turin Commission actually began its work – work finally made available to the English-speaking world in 1976, when David commissioned the translation of the Italian report. It was only then, with *The Silent Witness* production unit again acting as catalyst, that investigators throughout the world began to have some idea of what had been undertaken. For the first time it became widely known that permission had actually been granted for a handful of scientists to have a close, uninterrupted look at the Shroud which had obsessed so many of them for so long.

One waits with them through that tense moment, lost now in another decade receding ... The scrape of a ladder on stone, the low clatter of keys, the sibilance of distant echoes; the creak of a lock, a hinge; outside, the gathering heat of a summer day, the endless groaning of traffic past the city's grey arcades. The ornate grille, the chest, the casket – one by one the defences were opened. Then the reverential unrolling, the long linen at last revealed, its image, faint yet clear, precise yet shadowy, detailed yet spectral, at the mercy of an educated curiosity. The priests, the professors, the experts – eleven people in all – craned and shuffled, reduced for a moment to tourists, to children ...

It was four years later that, substantially the same in membership and its research requests agreed to, the Commission met again. Winter, now; November, and the Shroud on show to the world, not as before only to those who could make their way to Turin and crowd into the hall where it was displayed, but as things are put on show in the twentieth century, through television. Yet, despite this ferment of interest, the work of the Commission remained unannounced, unknown. No television reporter, no ecclesiastical correspondent was there to describe the scene as, in a small cathedral chamber, one of the four nuns who had been assigned the task drew the first sample thread from that ancient linen.

Seventeen such samples were taken from the Shroud, from various parts selected during the 1969 survey. From his permanent exile, Umberto had given his royal and Savoyard assent, stipulating only that the threads, once analysed, should be returned to Turin. More reluctantly, one imagines, he had also agreed that two small sections should be cut from the Shroud's edges, each of about four sq. cms.; the nuns removed these, then stitched the small wounds. Each sample, handled with tweezers, was placed in a tiny plastic envelope as soon as it had been removed. The intervention of so contaminating an agent as the human hand – even, alas, a nun's – had, of course, to be avoided. Only the material of the Shroud itself should be submitted to the Cyclopean probing of the microscope.

A particularly mysterious element has always been the medium that actually produces the marks on the Shroud. For centuries people assumed it to be blood (except for those who believed the cloth a forgery and thought it some kind of pigment). It was the task of the Commission to try and discover, as a preliminary to any further investigation, whether or not this actually was blood.

At the University of Turin, threads from the Shroud were examined under an ordinary high-magnification microscope. Professor Guido Filogamo noted nothing of interest except the presence of reddish granules of various shapes and sizes. It is of these unidentifiable units that the Shroud image seems to be constituted. Professor Filogamo and his assistant, Dr Alberto Zina, now fixed the threads in a resin which, hardening, enabled them to cut their specimens into slices down to one twenty thousandth of a millimeter thick. The optical microscope revealed nothing of any significance; to everyone's intense chagrin the electron microscope, despite its much greater powers of enlargement, produced results no more decisive. There were bacterial and other organic spores and debris, but these, of course, were only to be expected on material so many centuries old. The red-brown granules, however, continued to defy all examination. That these were the red globules which would have signified dried blood, report the scientists, 'cannot be excluded with absolute certainty' – but, they continued, their characteristics and appearance 'make such a possibility improbable'. They point out that attempts to study in such a way blood traces of any kind 'rarely produce positive results after a relatively short time', but this elaboration of a negative does not take them any further towards explaining what the mysterious granules actually are.

While Filogamo had had only two threads to work with, a three-professor team at Modena University had ten, the longest nearly thirty millimeters, the shortest only four. The team was headed by Professor Giorgio Frache (nominally, at least; the professor was ill for part of the time), a forensic scientist with a well-equipped laboratory. The first result, from the most straightforward examination under the microscope, was perhaps the most interesting. 'At the level of the zones which also appeared darker to the naked eye, the surface fibres take on a more intense colouring, a fairly uniform reddish colour. This colouring is found only on the surface fibres, so much so that the above-mentioned colouring was only observed on the reverse of the thread at the level of the underlying fibres by transparency.' In other words, the stains that formed the image had not penetrated the material at all. They had not, as one would have expected, changed the colouration of the whole thread. Indeed, in order to see the stain at all from the underside of the thread, one had to focus a light intense enough to render the material semi-transparent. Every thread so examined showed the same characteristics. The image on the Shroud was strictly a surface phenomenon.

How strictly was not really appreciated until the threads, their fibres teased apart with a histological needle, were examined at an enlargement of 285 diameters. The reddish-brown granules of which the stains were composed were clearly visible. 'These granulations affected the majority of the fibres, indeed substantially so, but they were not found in the spaces between the fibres.' Whatever their composition, it seemed less and less likely that they had been left behind by a flow of blood, however long ago. Liquids, whether through capillary attraction or the force of gravity, tend to cling equally to every part of a fibre; automatically, they fill in the spaces between one fibre and the next.

Under ultra-violet light, the derivatives of haemoglobin, the red pigment of the blood, have a tendency to fluoresce. In this case, however, 'The examination showed negative results'. Surely aware by now that this would be the story throughout the rest of the investigation, the scientists nevertheless set about discovering the reaction of the stains to benzidine. This is a colourless substance which, reacting to a catalyst present in haemoglobin, turns blue on contact with blood. It is very useful as a test in old criminal cases and in historical research, because the peroxidase which acts as the catalyst has a strong resistance to the passage of time. Again the results were negative: 'Careful examination did not show any change of colour to blue, either at the level of the bulk of the granules or in the combination of the fibre'. As they had already pointed out in their report, 'A negative result ...

allows us to exclude that in the material under examination there are traces of blood still demonstrable'.

Using spectroscopy, Professor Frache's team tested for haemochromogen – "a derivative of haemoglobin frequently found in marks of an ancient date' – but they found none. They made chromatographic tests, with no better fortune. They were forced to conclude that 'the results of the investigation in the laboratory of forensic medicine ... would tend to exclude the presence of blood, even of the slightest traces ...' They had, however, already warned 'that researches by generic and specific diagnoses of blood on material of a very ancient date ... can have a real probative import only if the results are positive. In effect, the specific proteins of the blood, and of the relative pigment, if subjected ... to processes of degeneration or decay, can lose the characteristics which allow identification'. In other words the Shroud was so old that only a positive result counted. Blood was certainly present if you could prove that it was; if you could not prove it, however, that might mean no more than that the proofs had vanished down the centuries.

The tests had, nevertheless, been far from a waste of time and effort. They had established what later examination confirmed – that the image on the Shroud does not penetrate to the other side of the fabric, or even any distance into its texture. In the course of the tests, the granules had been exposed to treatment by various chemicals and acids. They had remained largely resistant to all of them; they had not dissolved and they had hardly changed colour. What this suggested was that the image had not been created by any normal colouring agent, whether natural or man-made. Such pigments are usually organic – they certainly were in the fourteenth century and before – and, originally spread in solution, dissolve once more when brought into contact with fluids. They are usually extremely responsive to chemicals and acids. They fill in the cracks and crevices of the surfaces they cover. They seep through, or at least into, any textiles on which they are used. They had not been used, it was probably safe to conclude, for the image that covered the Holy Shroud.

On the other hand, the fact that no blood was present made the image even more mysterious. And what were those strange red-brown granules? How had they been formed? How, once formed, had they been distributed across the linen? If they had not been in solution, how had they been spread? By some process that required no fluid? What was that process? Had Vignon been right? Or would scientists seventy years later be able to offer some new and more acceptable explanation? When serious investigation grapples with a profound problem, the results tend to throw up many questions rather than answers.

While these tests had been under way in Italy, in Belgium, the material of the Shroud was itself the subject of experimentation. Professor Gilbert Raes, of the Ghent Institute of Textile Technology, had been given four samples: two threads and the two tiny pieces of linen. That it was, in fact, linen he established in his first tests. Illuminating his samples with polarised light to increase contrast, Professor Raes examined them under the microscope. Their structure was typical and clear to see. There would be no surprises here.

What was something of a surprise, however, was that on specimens he had prepared, 'originating from the warp as well as the weft of the material, one observed traces of cotton fibre. It seemed that the linen threads had been spun in a place where one also spun cotton'. Raes seized on the cotton, to see what clues it might provide. He was looking to see how many twists or 'reversals' there were in every centimeter of thread, for these are features that vary with the type of cotton. 'For the cotton fibres found in the linen thread the number of reversals is around 8 per cm., which corresponds to the variety *Herbaceum*. This kind of cotton already existed in the Middle East.'

That linen and cotton were worked on the same

machinery causes one little surprise. "Ye shall keep my statutes", the Lord tells his people in *Leviticus*, and adds that "thou shalt not sow thy field with mingled seed: neither shall a garment mingled of linen and woollen come upon thee". Mixtures of this kind were frowned on in Jewish orthodoxy – but cotton, spreading westward from the Indus Valley, arrived too late to be included in an oral tradition that stretched back to the second Millenium BC. Thus the *Mishna*, the code of conduct regulating the day-to-day behaviour of practicing Jews, although written down perhaps three centuries later than was *Leviticus*, continues to prohibit the mixing of linen and wool but has nothing to say about cotton. As had happened so often, the Shroud had circumvented a potential negative which, if proven, would have destroyed its claims to authenticity. The circumvention, however, proved nothing of itself. The material of the Shroud was not ruled out as a Jewish product by the mixture that Professor Raes had discovered, but this did not go one step toward proving that it actually *was* a Jewish product.

Equally the weave itself, with its herringbone patterning, could have been produced in the Middle East during the first century. Such work was more commonly seen in silks, but it was seen and there was no reason why it should not have appeared in a good-quality linen. This logical block to all positive affirmation is to be seen in the professor's own conclusions. As he tells us, "One may say that there is no precise indication available permitting one to affirm with certainty that the material does not date from the time of Christ. It is also true, however, that nothing allows one to assert that the material in question was actually fabricated at that time."

One interesting fact Professor Raes did discover. The cotton fibres he had found clung only to threads from the main body of the Shroud. Samples taken from a long strip of matching linen sewn to one side included no cotton at all. The conclusion had to be that it had been woven at a different time. If that were so, it seemed a plausible assumption that it had been added at a later period by someone who wanted to match the texture and appearance of the main cloth. Just as Max Frei's findings had given support to Ian Wilson's general theory, so this evidence added credence to one portion of it. It was Wilson's conviction that the Shroud had been folded in four when, as the Image of Edessa, it had first dazzled Byzantium. To the people of Edessa, indeed, it had always been a portrait. It had almost certainly been presented to them and their king as such, in that distant time before persecution had caused it to be hidden and the memory of it had faded from the city. But why had it not been offered to Abgar and his subjects as the Shroud of Jesus? Wilson's thesis is that this had been impossible at a period when graveclothes were considered fundamentally unclean – especially those of a convicted and crucified man, however holy. One could not offer such a gift to a king. Diplomatically, therefore, the Shroud had been folded to show only the head. Thus curtailed, however, it must have looked unsettlingly off-centre, and it was for this reason that a side-piece had been sewn on. Now Raes had shown that the side-piece certainly was a later addition. Again, this proved nothing positive – but the fact that these findings did not *disprove* the theory meant that it had cleared another hurdle.

In addition to the scientific reports, the Turin Commission also included the educated suppositions of two North Italian experts. One was the Associate Professor of Egyptology at the University of Turin, Silvio Curto. As his Chair indicates, Professor Curto specialised in Egyptian antiquities, and he warns against assuming too close a parallel between the culture of Egypt and that of the Hebrews. Both Mesopotamia and the Graeco-Roman world had connections with first-century Palestine which falsified any assumption that Egypt must be our only, or even our main, source of information about life in the land where Jesus preached.

Professor Curto's report is a little indeterminate, as is

inevitable in what can only be the extended speculations of a knowledgeable mind. Asked to make archaeological observations on both the Shroud and its image, he raises a number of issues. He wonders, for example, why there is no mention of the Shroud in the Gospels. He considers what the reaction of Mary Magdalen, St Peter and the others was likely to have been to a cloth, found in that place at that time and marked with the imprint of Jesus's body. He thinks it a little strange that nothing was written about it, 'in view of the fact that the various records of what happened immediately after the burial relate in great detail even the most trivial events'.

He also considers it a problem – as indeed it is – that in the history of the Shroud there should be such long gaps, such periods of silence. Of course, if Ian Wilson's theories are correct, then these gaps are nothing like as long or quite as silent as Professor Curto believes; nevertheless, there is only the wispiest circumstantial evidence to link Mandylion with Shroud. For a century and a half we have no word of it, nor any evidence of where it has been. Again, Ian Wilson's theories are more than plausible, but they hardly add up to proof. Professor Curto is right to insist that at this point the attempt to authenticate the Shroud faces considerable problems.

The Professor then considers the Shroud material, but here has little of relevance to say; the researches of Professor Raes, as Curto himself implies, are more precisely to the point. He is somewhat uncertain about whether twill of the kind of which the Shroud was woven already existed in the Middle East during the relevant period but can be definite only about whether it was known in Egypt. When he considers the image, Professor Curto dismisses a number of possible alternatives to its creation 'by an event which would be impossible in the natural way'. He has strong objections to explanations of the kind favoured by Vignon, insisting that 'even a simple, superficial examination shows this interpretation to be completely unreal'. The fact that the back view is of the same density as the front, although the body will have touched it almost along its whole length, and the undistorted nature of the front view, although the cloth must have lain, curved, about or over the body, seems to him to rule out its having been 'produced by unguents and the issue of sweat, blood or similar substances, or else of evaporation from the fabric of internal organic substances or of unguents'. The fact that, although St John tells us that the head was wrapped, it appears as clear as any other part of the body, and the reversed nature of the image itself seem to him additional refutations.

That it was painted seemed, and seems, quite out of the question. No test has offered the slightest evidence that the Shroud image is in that sense man-made. But might it have been printed in some way, probably by the use of wooden blocks? On the whole, Professor Curto appears to incline to this view – 'if we accept this supposition', he writes, 'we cannot say that the style of the figure is of the late-ancient period, because of the psychology expressed in the face and the perfect anatomical details: consequently, due to the fact that the transfixion of the wrists could only have resulted from observations made during the 13th century or later, it could have been produced almost at any time after that'. This is a conclusion which seems to ignore the question of pigmentation: The unlikelihood implicit in the results of the microscopic examination, that paint or pigment has ever been on the Shroud must also apply to inks and dyes. Those almost indestructable red-brown granules need firmer refutation that Professor Curto's, 'In Christian Persia there was a legend according to which Christ adolescent had worked in a dye-house and was therefore considered patron of dyers'.

The same problem faces another hypothesis offered in the Turin Commission's report, that of Professor Noemi Gabrielli. As the former Director of the Piedmontese art galleries, she had been brought in to place the Shroud to the general history of art. Her suggestion was 'that the author's model was not engraved on a wooden block ...

but drawn by the author directly onto a wet cloth stretched on a frame, using a compound of sepia-coloured clay and yellow ochre diluted in a resinous liquid, and that this original, while still wet, was then spread out over the Shroud, also well stretched, and pressed against it with a padded weight, as used to be done for printing'. The advantage of this theory, she claimed, was that it explained the 'negative' effect of the image – the positive of the original design became reversed in the subsequent transfer – as well as the absence of the distortions that might otherwise have been expected. As to who was responsible, she says categorically, 'It is the work of a great artist of the late fifteenth and early sixteenth centuries, who used the Leonardo technique of shading. If we compare the Shroud with the face of Christ in the Last Supper we find a similarity in the technique and spirituality.' She asserts that the Shroud now in Turin must have been created some 130 years later than that displayed by Geoffrey de Charny and that the artist responsible, 'with his thorough knowledge of anatomy, would appear to have transfused into his canvas his geniality and the emotional turmoil of his soul ...' It should be 'considered a masterpiece of figurative art'.

By thus blithely both rewriting history and ignoring the scientific evidence, she makes out a case for the Shroud's having been created by a Renaissance genius as great as Leonardo da Vinci or – half-hinted at – by Leonardo himself. She has suggested, of course, the only man with the blend of artistic ability, technical ingenuity and psychological insight who might plausibly have forged so powerful an icon. She offers no evidence to support her notion, however. She lists other holy cloths claimed to be the shroud of Jesus, most long vanished, some of the copies that were made of these and the artists who painted them. Nowhere, however, does she link the general possibility of forgery, which has always been present, with particular evidence proving that *this* Shroud is spurious.

Professor Gabrielli also returns to the historical

arguments that seventy years earlier had isolated the scientific work of Paul Vignon. She cites the opposition of Peter d'Arcis and quotes one or two sour descriptions of the Shroud as proof that the image has changed over the centuries. For example she passes on to us the opinion of one Rupis, secretary late in the fifteenth century to the Duke of Mantua. He described the Shroud, exhibited in 1494, as 'a sheet in which the body of our Lord was wrapped before being laid in the tomb and on which his image can be seen outlined in blood – both front and back – and it looks as though the blood is still issuing'. She declares categorically, 'it would appear that the Turin Shroud cannot be one and the same as that seen by Rupis'; given the circumstances of pomp and reverence in which Rupis must have seen the Shroud, and the awe he and his companions will doubtless have felt, it seems slightly wilful to consider this so bad a description that it must refer to some quite different cloth.

These, then, were the main elements in the Turin Commission's report. This often contradictory collection of hard scientific evidence and soft academic opinion had been issued in 1976 as an appendix to the Turin diocesan magazine. There had been no attempt to publicise it or to submit its findings to the critical scrutiny of the world intellectual community. In its grey paper covers and its scholarly Italian, it would have remained inaccessible or unknown to many but the most dedicated experts. It was David Rolfe who, with funds from the finances of *The Silent Witness*, arranged to have it translated into English and circulated to interested scientists. Once again he and his film had acted as a catalytic agent in Shroud researches, creating new elements and combinations in a situation which without them would have remained largely static. At the same time, he was widening the scope of the film itself. No longer propagating only the ideas of Ian Wilson, *The Silent Witness* was turning into a summary of all contemporary research into the authenticity of the Shroud. More than that, it was engendering research; in the case of Max Frei, for example, it had been at least a partial sponsor. Both David and the film had developed a good deal since that pregnant moment when, from the floor, where it had fallen, the brooding, pain-marked face of the Shroud image had first stared up at him.

CHAPTER SIX

A moment of truth was approaching, a time when all the hopes, all the work planned or accomplished, all the researching, the reading, the travelling, the talking would be drawn together into a single decision. Until now, David had been busy with what were essentially the preliminaries; soon, however, it would be necessary for him to show a script to Harry John and, like a counsel with his case argued, await the verdict. Was the Foundation prepared to add, to the sums already disbursed, the much larger amounts needed for the actual production? Would *The Silent Witness* at last be filmed?

He decided that for the preparation of the final version of the script, the one he was actually going to shoot from, he needed a hand more expert and experienced than Wilson's. He chose as his additional writer Henry Lincoln, a man with a number of film and television credits to his name, who had shown in the past that he could make instantly gripping on the screen the oddities of history. For a project of his own, Lincoln had even made an investigation of the Knights Templar and their vanished treasure. In many respects, therefore, he seemed the ideal choice. Even Ian Wilson, understandably disturbed at the time by this move, later came to accept its necessity.

Lincoln's real work, however, could not begin until David knew whether or not the project was to continue. He prepared a detailed outline, the kind of preliminary script that film people call a treatment. In it, the basic shape of the intended film was made clear: an investigation, taking the story stage by stage, into the background and authenticity of the Shroud. The experience of watching it should, David felt, be akin to that of seeing a thriller, a detective story. One by one the relevant clues would be examined and their significance made plain. At the end, he hoped that his audiences would at least be able to arrive at some sort of conclusion. They might never be able to achieve absolute certainty, but they should leave the cinemas or television screens with no doubts as to the seriousness and validity of the claims made.

In order to guarantee the final stages of preparation, David had to pack his bags and once more set out across the Atlantic. To the Holy Shroud Guild and the De Rance Foundation he had to justify what he had done so far, what he proposed doing and the people he had chosen to help him do it. If he could survive this particular obstacle, then nothing faced him until he submitted the final script for Harry John's approval.

Early in December, 1976, he saw again the hallucinatory towers of Manhattan, gleaming under a grey sky as he was whirled along the freeway from Kennedy Airport. He stood once more in those endless avenues, feeling this time the keen edge of the unimpeded wind. Father Rinaldi and Father Otterbein – the latter having travelled from Miami especially for his visit – made him welcome; there was developing between them now that comfortable friendship that can exist between associates who agree on the value of their joint project. They liked David's approach, liked his idea of the shape the film should take, approved of his associates. They advanced a name of their own – Dr Robert Bucklin of Los Angeles. He was a forensic pathologist working with that city's police department, and had for many years shown a deep interest in the anatomical evidence of the Shroud image. He was the ideal person to offer a medical testimony.

A pause beside the iron-grey waters of Lake Michigan to meet Dr McCrone of Chicago and discuss the possibility of using carbon-dating techniques on the Shroud, an inconclusive meeting; then on up the lakeside to Milwaukee and the De Rance Foundation. Again the security checks, again the rumpled figure of the millionaire, improbable in his office setting, but this time a much more friendly examination of David's information. And indeed Mr John liked his outline, approved his approach – but offered one proviso. In what he had written there was no mention of Monsignor Ricci. The film could not be made without mentioning Monsignor Ricci's work. The Monsignor should be consulted. He was the world's foremost authority on the Shroud and could not be excluded. Mr John held the warmest feelings of friendship and respect for Monsignor Ricci. He insisted that David and Monsignor Ricci should meet, and as soon as possible.

David had relied on hearsay in his evaluation of Ricci's work. It seemed to him to be more a case of a theological interpretation – and one that occasionally ran ahead of the facts – than a scientific investigation. Harry John, however, felt that the analyses Ricci had made of the Shroud and its image covered every aspect open to the examining eye. His books were both fascinating and penetrating. He had to be included. David agreed to travel as soon as possible to Rome and see how Monsignor Ricci might fit into the general scheme.

With this, Harry John was satisfied. Indeed, the only problem that really disturbed everyone at this stage was the condition of the pound sterling, which was fluctuating unpredictably, mostly in a downward direction. It would make location filming, especially in the United States, much more expensive than had at one time seemed likely. To pour dollars into a fund that was instantly converted into sterling, and then to see that sterling steadily lose value until the day when it had to be converted back into dollars again, seemed a peculiarly wasteful way to finance the film. No millionaire could be expected to feel easy about it. David decided to ask Treasury permission to set up a dollar account from which to draw his overseas expenses.

There remained one further meeting, with Dr

Gallagher, Harry John's right-hand man, a slow-moving, taciturn man. Before he had joined Harry John, no one had lasted in the post for more than a year or so. He had been in it for twenty-five years. Asked about Harry John he replies indulgently, 'Well, he's grown up like a king. No one ever says no to him.' He stares reflectively over one's shoulder. 'I've been with him twenty-five years – and I've argued with him a couple of times.' His expression mixes pride with sheepishness. He is, nevertheless, acute, wry, self-deprecating, with an intelligence only partly dulled by the sycophantic nature of his employment. With David he went through the production's account and, more importantly, accounting procedures and was satisfied with both.

His first action was to meet Dr Bucklin, the Los Angeles pathologist, a tall, lanky man, with a long-jawed Yankee face rimmed by an almost over-neat white beard. The medical examiner took him to his place of work, the City Morgue. Amid the endless distracted traffic of smog-wreathed Los Angeles, this was perhaps the quietest place in town. For the first time, David had the unsettling experience of being surrounded by the dead.

Dr Bucklin, however, proved to be precisely the kind of controlled, knowledgeable witness David had been searching for. He decided he would film him there, amid the hygienic tiles and glaring lights, the deep whisperings of the refrigerated drawers, and the endless ranks of rubber-tyred stretchers with their marble-white, marble-still relays of the dead. It would place the man in his gruesome but efficient context and let the long experience it implied lend its weight to what he said. David spoke with the authorities. He found them enthusiastically cooperative, perhaps because of Dr Bucklin's impressive credentials, perhaps because Los Angeles is a city of film-makers. All their facilities, they said, would be placed at the disposal of David and his film crew.

David returned from the West Coast to Colorado Springs, where at the US Air Force Academy John

Jackson and Eric Jumper, both Captains and both Assistant Professors, had for some time been engaged in a private research programme of their own into the nature of the Shroud and its image. Both in their early thirties, they had begun their work while at the Jet Propulsion Laboratories at Pasadena, California. Transferred to the Air Force Academy, they had left behind them a little group eager to continue the work they had started.

They were both experts in the use of computerised forms of scanning, through which ordinary photographs may be induced to give up all kinds of information not apparent to the naked eye. They were slowly compiling new information, derived from these and similar techniques, about the Shroud. The scientific credentials they brought to their voluntarily accepted task were impressive; as for the techniques, they had been developed for and tested in the space programme. Jackson and Jumper were now eager to present their own findings and collate them with those of other experts, theological and historical as well as scientific. In order to do so, they were organising a conference to be held in Albuquerque the following Spring, at which the details of Shroud research were to be brought fully up to date at a series of seminars, meetings and addresses.

David got on very well with these young scientists. They were more or less of the same generation as he, married and with young children, as he was, and he could be at ease with them in a way that he sometimes found difficult with some of his other collaborators. They were appreciative, as scientists, of his determination to make his film objective; as men who had given months of their spare time to their Shroud researches, they warmed to his refusal to allow commercial demands to distort this intention. As a result, not only did they invite him most warmly to attend the Albuquerque Conference, they also agreed that film and television exposure of their work should be exclusively through *The Silent Witness*.

David flew back to New York in a mood of considerable

satisfaction. To the theories of Ian Wilson he had now been able to add the expert testimony of Max Frei, John Jackson and Eric Jumper, the cooperation of the Holy Shroud Guild and, through them, the medical evidence of Dr Robert Bucklin. He had ensured that the energising funds of the De Rance Foundation would continue to flow through the veins of his project. In England, a final script was under way. Out of his amazed reaction to that first flimsy manuscript, he had constructed a venture with world-wide ramifications. After a brief meeting with Father Rinaldi – benign as ever and almost as enthusiastic as he – David flew back across the Atlantic.

He did not stay long in Britain, however. He could no longer postpone the visit to Monsignor Ricci in Rome on which Harry John had insisted. After Christmas, therefore, David took his wife and daughter on the first organised holiday they had ever been able to afford; invigorated by two weeks' skiing in the Italian Alps, he saw them off on their return journey and then travelled down to Turin to meet Don Coero, the secretary of the International Centre for Sindonology. This organisation, originally set up by the owners of the Shroud, the House of Savoy, coordinates and collates the research work being carried out all over the world, in science, history and philosophy, on the Shroud. Some of this work it publishes itself, in the multi-lingual quarterly, *Sindon*, full of erudite articles on this or that aspect of the Holy Shroud – its origins, its various owners, its antiquity, its significance.

Don Coero, a short, jovial man of unobtrusive charm and great energy, supervises all this activity from a small back room not much more enticing than a wardrobe. Tucked under a staircase, it holds a small desk, a hard chair, rows of files grey with dust; on the desk there is a single telephone. An unostentatious man, exuding friendliness and a desire to help. He offered David the use of a rare book of illustrations, prepared for the 1933 exhibition, in which representations of all the Shroud's public displays throughout its history had been gathered together. He gave permission for Secondo Pia's original camera to be used in the film, in the actual surroundings where that historic first photograph had been taken. He showed David the original casket in which the Shroud had been brought to Turin from Chambéry, and displayed the sombrely ornate uniform and insignia of the Order of the Holy Shroud, once in the gift of Italy's royal family. He arranged for David to meet Monsignor Caramello, appointed by Cardinal Pellegrino to be responsible for the safety of the Shroud, who had been the chairman of the Turin Commission of 1969-73.

Delighted with the cooperation he had been both given and promised, David took the night train for Rome. The Rome centre was very different from that in Turin. The luxurious building housed a large library, a classroom where Monsignor Ricci taught those who wanted to learn about his views on the Shroud, and a sitting-room in which to entertain important visitors; there was an imposing office with a pleasant view from the windows, there was even a large terrace on which chairs and swinging garden seats stood invitingly among a disciplined profusion of flowering shrubs.

Monsignor Ricci was charming and friendly, his mellifluous voice never displaying the slightest acerbic note. Yet he was far from offering the unconditional cooperation of Don Coero. He made it clear that his connection with Harry John gave him the right to overlook the contents of the film. His, he implied, would be the supervisory capacity. Not only this, he added: his Centre expected to be well rewarded for his participation, the sum he mentioned being £12000. If these conditions were not met, it was hinted not only would he take no part in the film, he would use his influence with Mr John to see that there was no film.

David faced an acute dilemma. Monsignor Ricci's stand seemed to be underwritten by the financial authority of Harry John. Yet if he gave way now, the whole character of the film would alter. For example, it was based on Ian

Wilson's research – yet the Monsignor did not approve of or agree with Wilson's conclusions. If Ricci had his way, Wilson's work would be censored out of existence. If he did not have his way, however, he would withdraw and very probably take Harry John with him. The first possibility meant that the film would not be worth making, the second that it could not be made.

David's first commitment was to Ian Wilson. It was upon his original manuscript that the whole venture was based. Over two years of effort had gone into building on those foundations. He had no intention now of destroying the very ground on which he stood. He decided to temporise, to agree to everything that he could, to seem to accept what he would finally reject, to seem to believe what he actually doubted, to smile and nod where actually he wanted to shake his fists and yell curses. It was a course of action that, misunderstood by Wilson, was later to cause considerable friction with him. A temporiser by necessity, David was caught in the crossfire of absolutists. If he had failed, he would have been accused of weakness; as he succeeded, we must say that with a great deal of aplomb and to everyone's eventual satisfaction, he played the diplomat. In short, he behaved like a film producer.

One can sense the underlying tension in the report David wrote at the time. Intended for all the interested parties, it had to be accurate, believable, bland, optimistic, uncontentious. It had to be truthful without telling the truth, comprehensive in subject matter, but evasive in analysis. For those who knew something of the actual situation, the strains must have been evident and the results not without humour.

'Monsignor Ricci expressed some slight reservations about the work of Ian Wilson ... he did not think the Shroud and the Image of Edessa were the same but nevertheless would be prepared to revise his opinion should Wilson's evidence be convincing enough. I emphasised that where elements were not beyond genuine scholastic dispute this would be reflected in the film ... I had already explained that, mainly because of the unavailability of English language translations of Monsignor Ricci's work, I had little knowledge of its extent. Also what knowledge I did have had been gleamed from English scholars whose own views were sometimes at variance with it and was therefore slightly hampered in giving a purely objective opinion. In Monsignor Ricci's own apartment, surrounded by the material collected over the twenty-six years of his research, I watched a full visual presentation of his findings narrated by Monsignor Ricci himself ...'

Nevertheless, Ricci's work on the physical details of the Shroud image, and the meticulous way he had related these to the story of the Passion, opened out the possible treatment of these matters in the film. David saw in these findings a way to persuade his backer to fund a dramatic reconstruction of the crucifixion – Harry John would agree if he felt that the full demonstration of Monsignor Ricci's work demanded it. He wrote, 'I had previously felt that there was not sufficient research available for the film to justify a scientific reconstruction of the manner and cause of death of the man on the Shroud. Monsignor Ricci's presentation, however, showed me clearly that this was not so.'

Most scientists, nevertheless, did not accept Monsignor Ricci's findings. He drew enormous conclusions from the flimsiest evidence, basing himself not only on an *a priori* acceptance of the Shroud image as that of Jesus, but also on a kind of theological sentimentality unattractive to the layman. Aware of this, David pointed out that 'several aspects of Monsignor Ricci's reconstruction of the anatomy of the body and how the cloth was wrapped around it were at direct variance with other scientific theories I had recently encountered and yet could obviously not be dismissed ... At the same time, it was also evident that the other theories themselves had strong points not completely countered, at this point.' David suggested that Monsignor Ricci should attend the

Albuquerque Conference, intended to resolve precisely those differences that divided other Shroud theoreticians from him. For the Vatican expert, who had not yet heard of the proposed meeting, this seemed an excellent idea.

David showed him the proposals he had outlined for the film. 'Monsignor Ricci could see that its scope was purely geared to cover the question of authenticity and accepted it as such. I also believe he could see some merit in its "detective" approach and style. In his own words, however, although he recognised that such a film was essential, in its own right, to establish the fascinating case for authenticity, such a film would ... "be but a frame for a picture of the meaning of the Shroud ...", an area which I believe his own work covers in detail and is unique.'

Having taken his appreciation so far, David pounced. 'Given the very scholatic nature of the film', he wrote, 'any significantly questionable or unauthenticated reconstructions could jeopardise the integrity of the other materials. However ... my opinion on this has altered, having seen the extent and the very objective and mathematical basis of Monsignor Ricci's work in this field, particularly in relation to the flagellation and facial wounds, as well as the reconstruction of the precise details of the crucifixion ... My proposal is that we add to the basic filming programme a detailed dramatic sequence depicting the conclusion of the trial of Jesus, the scourging, the journey to the cross and the actual crucifixion as reconstructed from the Shroud by Monsignor Ricci.' In other words, the high regard Harry John had for Ricci was a lever David would use to widen the scope of the film. If this was what was needed to tempt the hand that held the purse-strings into munificence, then this is what David would do. 'This proposal', he added carefully, 'will of course, affect the budget as it would be essential to film the sequence with great care ... the extra expenses could be justified by the fact that, as Monsignor Ricci has pointed out, after one has overcome the hurdle of authenticity, there is a natural progression to a film on the meaning and significance of the image on the Shroud.' Of such devious diplomacy is woven the success of producers – perhaps after all the students at the Film School had been correct in their assessment of these gentry. So David thought, contemplating the dubious manoeuvres into which he was being led. 'Monsignor Ricci and I parted in very good spirit', he wrote in counterfeit euphoria, 'having achieved, I believe, a good rapport over the subject generally. I had been extremely impressed by the value and detail of his work and the highly objective and open-minded approach he had to it.' And what else could he have said? That Monsignor Ricci had tried to establish himself as the sole arbiter of authenticity? That he shared the scholarly doubts that had been expressed by some about the value of the Monsignor's work? He might have congratulated himself upon his honesty – but would that have compensated him for the loss of his film?

So, throughout his days in Rome, David smiled and smiled, talked, agreed, debated, offered courtesies, smiled, made suggestions, respectful proposals, deferential plans, smiled – and outlined the terms of a contract. There was, of course, discussion, the chamber warfare of civilised opposition, but in the end Monsignor Ricci signed. It may be that, at the moment of choice, he could not after all bear to be excluded. In any case, he accepted a fee – still for his Centre, naturally; not for himself – of something like a quarter the sum he had first demanded. More importantly, there was no mention of his having any control over the film's contents: David had preserved his freedom. (This did not prevent Monsignor Ricci later claiming to the Turin Centre that *The Silent Witness* would be 'his' film, thus for a considerable time alienating Don Coero.)

As he ate with Monsignor Ricci and his sister in their agreeable apartment or returned that hospitality with a dinner in his hotel, and later, as he flew home again, David was sustained by the conviction that he had gathered another member to his team. He was to prove by no means the easiest member, but he had done meticulous work on the Shroud, he appeared to be the preferred expert of the Vatican and – in this context, above all – he had won the slightly unpredictable respect of Harry John. Remembering the jovial modesty of Don Coreo, however, David could not help wishing that it was in Turin that the original work had been done. He contrasted the glitter of the Rome centre with the dust and poverty of the office in Turin the discernable self-esteem of the Monsignor with the energetic cooperation of the Turin priest, the offers of assistance he had had from the latter with the former's veiled assertion that, deeply in Harry John's confidence, it was his word that would finally decide the shape and content of the film.

Nevertheless, as he wrote his painfully careful report back in London, nothing could diminish his contentment. If his relationship with Ian Wilson was occasionally strained, if Monsignor Ricci threatened to take the whole venture over from within, if Harry John remained unsettlingly enigmatic, these were the very stuff of the work he had undertaken. The planning and the politics, the travelling and the conferring, the principled stands and the diplomatic evasions, the easy spending and the careful budgets – these were what made up that exciting totality, the production of a film. And his film would be produced. One day a screen would light up and proclaim to an attentive audience, *The Silent Witness*. It would have the structure and the integrity he had two years before decided it would. It would be his film. He was certain of it now.

CHAPTER SEVEN

Ever since scientists first began to take the Holy Shroud seriously, they have disagreed amongst themselves over some at least of their findings. Science, as Karl Popper has told us, works in an evolutionary manner, setting up hypotheses which do or do not survive according to their ability to withstand the prevailing critical environment. As weaker theories are eliminated, we come closer to the perfection of fact. The work that has been done on the Shroud is no exception; the problem has been to define the criteria by which the various theories and ideas should be judged. How was the image created? What critical apparatus can be brought to bear upon an event which appears to have occurred only once in human history?

Certainly there was the 'vapourograph' theory of Vignon. But there have also been experiments, and relatively successful experiments, with methods using direct contact and suggesting that the body must have touched the Shroud in order to mark it. Dr Judica-Cordiglia, Professor of Forensic medicine at Milan University and an investigator favoured by the ecclesiastical authorities, obtained his impression by impregnating a piece of linen with oil and essence of terebinth and spreading it over a body covered in blood. Another medical investigator, Dr Romanes, using powdered salt on the body to reproduce the effects of its chemical exudations and then steeped his simulacrum of the Shroud in powdered aloes. In both cases an image was certainly produced, although it lacked the precise detail of the Shroud.

The critical climate altered sharply with the publication of the Turin Commission's findings, in 1976. If the image was no more than a surface phenomenon, as it seemed to be, none of these suggested methods could be the right one, as each soaked into fabric; colour would have permeated all the affected threads. Whatever had caused the image, it was not a process involving a period of percolation, a slow imprinting, such as these theories demanded. Then what was it? What *had* caused this endlessly mysterious image? Shroud studies were once more in confusion.

There were other points of dispute. Some were relatively minor, like that involving the flow of 'water and blood' from the deep wound in the side. Barbet had thought this was pericardial fluid; Professor Mödder, a radiologist from Cologne, believed it to be fluid from the pleural sac; while, more recently, an American surgeon, Anthony Sava, had proposed that it was fluid that had collected, in the course of the brutalities inflicted on him, in the man's pleural cavity. This is something which occurs when the lungs themselves are bruised during an assault on the rib-cage.

In the light of some recent ill-informed claims that Jesus did not actually die on the cross, one of the most important debates concerned the probable cause of death. Barbet had suggested that the cause of death was asphyxiation, brought about when the body, slumping into an unnatural position from exhaustion, constricted the upper chest. Professor Mödder had modified this theory, however, basing his own ideas on a series of uncomfortable and even dangerous experiments in which he used himself and some of his students as subjects. They bound themselves to a bar in the crucifixion attitude, sometimes with their feet supported and sometimes not. When their feet were free, they became unconscious after six to twelve minutes; when they were supported it took longer. The cause was not respiratory, however, but due to a swift lowering of blood pressure. The medical term for the draining of blood to the lower limbs and its pooling there whenever for any reason the force of gravity overcomes the pumping power of the heart, is orthostatic collapse. It is this that Professor Mödder saw as the most likely cause of death – the heart and especially the brain were deprived of their essential blood supply. The English authority, Dr D. Willis, has supported Professor Mödder's theory and it now seems the most likely. Dr Sava, however, has, as will be seen, his own proposal to make on the matter.

The fact that there were such divergent ideas, and so many exploded theories leaving unanswered the problems they once purported to solve, was the reason why in 1977 Captains Jumper and Jackson, of the USAF, decided to organise a conference on the state of Shroud studies at which work done might be described and work proposed might be outlined. These were the officers, both professors at the Air Force Academy, whom David had already met in Colorado Springs, and brought as consultants into his *The Silent Witness* enterprise; eventually, they were to appear in the film. He had become enthusiastic about the conference, and not only contributed $2000 from his scanty finances to its cost, but also flew out at his company, Screenpro's, expense those British experts associated with the documentary. When, on 23 March, 1977, the delegates assembled in the thin, early-spring air of Albuquerque, New Mexico, for the first of their two days of lecture and debate, he like they was more than ready to be fascinated by what he would hear.

Father Otterbein spoke, about the Shroud and the Guild; Father Rinaldi described with approval how the attitudes of the Turin authorities to scientific research on the Shroud had become more relaxed and co-operative. Rev. David Sox discussed non-Catholic and even non-Christian interest in the Shroud: 'The Shroud has been a symbol of unity in the past', he said, 'when it was brought by the House of Savoy from Chambéry to Turin; it united the people to a new capital. The Shroud may again become a symbol of unity now that interest and research into its complexities have united men from various religious and philosophical backgrounds.' As if to exemplify his hopes, one of the early contributors was the Rt Rev. John Robinson, a Protestant, an Anglican, at one time Bishop of Woolwich and now Dean of Trinity College, Cambridge.

What had struck him was the fact that 'no forger starting, as he inevitably would, from the details of the Gospels, and especially that of the fourth, would have created the Shroud we have. Yet, *if* it were genuine, it must make us look again at the Biblical evidence'. There was, he said, 'multiple testimony for the tradition that the body of Jesus, released by Pilate at the request of Joseph of Arimathea, was taken from the cross late on Friday afternoon ...' It was placed in a prepared but as yet unused rock-tomb at dusk. The stars were beginning to appear, signalling the Passover Sabbath. Very little time remained in which the devout might do any work, even in the preparation of the dead for burial. Joseph had brought a *sindon*, a linen cloth, and in this he wrapped, according to Mark, or folded according to Matthew and Luke, the body of Jesus. There followed the application of myrrh and aloes, as described by John, although the quantities said to have been used may be an exaggeration. 'But', says Dr Robinson, 'there are parallels for such quantities, and if the mixture was packed under and around the sides of the body (perhaps thus explaining the flatness of the Shroud) a lot would have been needed.' Finally, the stone was rolled into the mouth of the tomb; so began the long wait over that otherwise celebratory week-end.

'So far there is no difficulty in correlating the Biblical evidence with that of the Shroud ... That the corpse of Jesus was enfolded in a simple linen cloth passing lengthwise over the head and covering the whole body back and front is not, I submit, what any forger with mediaeval or modern presuppositions would have thought of; but it makes complete sense of the texts and conforms with the other ancient evidence.' Thus, assertively, Dr

Robinson; but he goes on, 'It is when we come to the accounts of what was discovered on Easter morning that the problems begin.' He discusses the 'extraordinarily elusive' Greek in John's account of how the empty tomb was discovered: 'His expressions are so loose that it could mean that the clothes were lying strewn about with the napkin that had been over the head rolled up or bundled into a heap by itself ... But what does the evangelist intend us to suppose that the disciples did see?''

The problem is one of translation and interpretation. There is *sindon*, a linen cloth; *othonia*, which means grave-clothes, their material unspecified; these two words seem at times to be interchangeable. Then there is *suderion*, which is, Dr Robinson explains, 'a loan word from the Latin and defines the object not by its material (though clearly it was a cloth of some kind), but by its function, namely to wipe away sweat, rather like our handkerchief ... It seems in the highest degree improbable that it would be big enough to cover the length of a man twice.' These Greek words, well-known to the scribes who set them down and for them describing familiar objects, have tended to confuse modern attempts to relate the evidence of the Shroud with that of the Gospels. Dr Robinson, however, has his own proposal, based on a comparison between the accounts of Jesus's burial and Lazarus's raising. He says of these Bible stories that 'neither in the case of Lazarus nor in that of Jesus does it say that the *sudarion* covered the face. We are told that it was round the face of the former and over the head of the latter. The only position, I submit, which fits both these description ... is of something tied crossways over the head, round the face and under the chin. In other words, it describes a jaw-band ...' This would have to be applied, just as the eyes would have to be closed, before *rigor mortis* could set in.

What, Dr Robinson asks, did St John have in mind when describing the scene that met Mary Magdalene and, a little later, the disciple Peter? 'How a first century Jew would naturally have envisaged resurrection ... would surely have been as a corpse waking from sleep ... and then like Lazarus walking out of the tomb. The difference in the case of Jesus was that the grave-clothes did not need to be taken off him nor the stones removed: he did it himself ... Far from being viewed as helpless and naked, he would probably have been envisaged in robes of light ...'

'Finally', Dr Robinson asks, 'what difference would the evidence of the Shroud, if genuine, make?' He thinks, on the whole, it would make very little. It is, he points out, compatible with the Gospel story but adds nothing to it. It does not explain by what agency or whose hands the body was removed. It offers 'no knock-down proof of resurrection'. What it does do is to take us, as the Gospels do not, into the actuality of that tomb. 'It is a unique story, complete with exclusive pictures.' But neither to the majesty nor to the significance of Jesus can it add one iota.

Ian Wilson detailed his theories to an audience largely in the mood to accept them, and then Dr George Sava, an expert in forensic medicine, offered the first acerbic touch of scientific objectivity. As he said, of Dr Barbet, 'the writer's personal piety clouded the boundary between subjectivity and scientific medical appraisal'. Dr Sava's main concern is with the flow of fluids from the wound in the side and its connection with the cause of death. He quotes a Dr Le Bec, a colleague of Barbet in Paris, who wrote a pamphlet entitled *The Death on the Cross* in which he called the colourless liquid that welled out after the chest was pierced a 'pleural exudate' and expressed scepticism over the lance having entered the pericardium. In the light of his own opinions, Dr Sava calls this 'strangely interesting' but dismisses, with what seems a characteristic terseness, Le Bec's assertion that Jesus died of nervous exhaustion: 'In our day, medical certification of death from "nervous exhaustion" is not acceptable.'

He details the results of a questionnaire which he sent to several surgeons specialising in operations of the thorax.

These have led him to conclude that repeated blows on the chest wall may produce a bloody effusion in the chest without any significant external wounding, and that this fluid collects between the lungs and the chest wall, compressing the former. Because no air enters the chest cavity, clotting cannot take place; the fluids are, therefore still able to flow several hours after death. There is a separation of the fluid into lighter and heavier components, the darker and heavier sinking to the bottom of the cavity. Most significant of all, one might think, he says, 'Pleural effusion caused by trauma to the chest wall is ten times more common than pericardial effusion'. He goes on, very firmly, 'This is not merely theory, but is instead the experience of specialists who see a large number of cases of chest violence in the course of routine practice. There seems now to be no difficulty in appreciating how the progressive increase of fluid will surely usher in death, by smothering or asphyxiation.'

Dr Sava goes on to challenge Barbet's assertion that the lance wound would remain gaping, allowing the pericardial fluids to escape, and that he had demonstrated this tunnelling effect in his experiments. Dr Sava's own work, carried out on corpses less than twelve hours after death, showed something very different. 'Upon withdrawing the knife, it was not possible to locate on the surface of the lung any sign of the wound ... I saw no sign of the 'veritable tunnel which seemed so important in the analysis proposed by Barbet.' He explains the contradiction between his findings and those of the French doctor by the fact that he had 'the great advantage of experimenting with bodies whose tissues had not lost their resilience before the experiments were carried out.' Dr Barbet, as an old man, apparently tried to persuade him not to publish these findings, ostensibly because they could not be right. 'In all kindness to Dr Barbet', Dr Sava says, still acerbic twenty-five years after the meeting, 'I confess that such an attitude is far from scientific.'

A disagreement, expertly conducted, with other medical

opinion on where precisely the nails pierced the wrists ended Dr Sava's contribution. It was lively and enlivening; one can imagine the audience shifting at its conclusion, perhaps smiling a little, aware that they had heard, however faintly and however benignly wielded, the cracking of an intellectual whip. Equally exacting in its own meticulous approach to detail was the lecture given by Monsignor Ricci.

To his testimony on the flagellation included in *The Silent Witness*, Monsignor Ricci adds the results of a lifetime's painstaking examination. From the bloodflow around these tiny scars he deduces the position of the victim at various moments as the lashes hissed and curled about him. In similar detail, he takes his audience through the stages of the crucifixion, constantly referring back to the Gospel history and building between the verbal evidence of the Apostles and the pictorial evidence of the Shroud a total drama that will satisfy or not, according to one's assessment both of the testimony and of Monsignor Ricci's handling of it. For example, he will take up some reference in the Bible account and then, it seems, search the Shroud for confirmation. He quotes from John, '... and bowing his head he gave up his spirit', then tells us with unqualified certainty, 'This particular of the bowed head can clearly be shown for the Man on the Shroud. It is proved by the linear distance from the sterno-clavicular articulation to the rima oris, which is the typical distance in the case of a man with his head considerably bent ... Rigor mortis set in, fixing that position, now revealed by the Shroud ...'

Monsignor Ricci also has very precise ideas about the significance of the folds and tucks demonstrated by the Shroud: 'The international wrapping and tucking-in of the Shroud permitted the necessary conditions for the fusion of an imprint that is impressive but has some serious anatomical anomalies'. He goes on to suggest that experiment excludes from anatomical possibility certain measurements on the imprint: for example, 'from the lips to the wound of the left carpus 68 cm. (due to the tucking of the sheet around the hands, that were one over the other with the thumb bent inside the palm, and due to the tucking of the sheet between the right arm and the right side). This can be proved by the presence of the imprint of blood on the right rib-case and the interruption of flow of the blood trickles (on the right arm) that moves from the right wrist down to the elbow. The excessive length of the imprint is about 20 cm.'

Whether, amid all the imponderables that surround the creation of the Shroud image, one can actually base such minutely specific conclusions on what the cloth shows is left to Monsignor Ricci's readers and hearers to accept or reject. He himself, in his published work, has set out in great detail the significance of every line and stain upon the Shroud, and one must go along with him as far as one believes the evidence permits.

Probably the main scientific matter dealt with at the Albuquerque Conference concerns the work of John Jackson and Eric Jumper, and by Bill Mottern, an image enhancement expert from the Sandia Laboratory, on the computer analysis of the Shroud image. In presenting their largely technical findings, they took the precaution to call on the assistance as editor of Kenneth Stevenson, an instructor in English at the Air Force Academy; it was a sensible step to take, since the evidence of these likable young scientists only too frequently drowns in a morass of jargon. At Albuquerque, however, they began by putting the facts very clearly and simply.

'The image on the purported burial cloth of Jesus of Nazareth, called today the Shroud of Turin, possesses two notable characteristics. First, the image on the Shroud has the properties of a photographic negative ... Second, our computer research has shown that the Shroud image is additionally three-dimensional, in that information defining the spatial contours of Jesus's body are encoded in the varying intensity levels of the image ... This three-dimensionality was first alluded to by Vignon when he noted that the intensity of the image seemed to vary inversely with cloth-body distance. In Vignon's day, there was no way to quantitatively demonstrate this relationship. Today, however, we have highly sensitive image-recording equipment which allows us to test this hypothesis.'

They had found a volunteer of the right physical proportions to be the subject of their first experiment. He duplicated, as far as was possible, the characteristics of the man on the Shroud. With immense care they draped a cloth bearing a replica of the image over the subject until the features of one exactly matched those of the other. When their relative positions had been determined, two photographs were taken, one with the cloth in place, the other with it removed. From the second photograph, an exact drawing of the subject was taken, and on it were indicated the highest points the cloth had taken when lying on his body the 'ridge-line' of the Shroud. To measure cloth-body distances then presented no problems.

With an electronic instrument called a microdensitometer (in the newer scientific disciplines often the more innocuous the equipment, the more fearsome its name) they then measured the intensity of the image along the ridge-line. With these two measurements at their disposal – distance of body from cloth and density of image – they were able to plot on a graph the correlation between the two. From the resultant curve it was clear that the closer the cloth had approached the body, the more intense was the image, and that this was in direct and precise proportion to the cloth-body distance.

If they could calculate these distances along the ridge-line, they could do so at any other point they chose. They now 'converted all image points to vertical relief rather than just those image points of the ridge line'.

They were now ready to use yet another item in their armoury of electronic miracle workers. This is an instrument known as the VP-8 Image Analyzer. The firm that make it, Interpretation Systems, describe it with the happy volubility of a technocrat chatting to his peers, even when – perhaps especially when – his medium is a publicity leaflet. 'This versatile instrument operates on a video image input and converts the image data to new display formats for improved visual image interpretation and classification ... The capabilities of the VP-8 are varied and include isodensity contouring, image density measurement, signal level monitoring, 3D display, colour and monochrome presentation ...' It continues, in this language which is not quite English and not quite anything else, but the important phrase has already come and gone. '3D display' – feed in a two-dimensional image which contains usable information about the third, and the VP-8 will display it on a television screen in those three dimensions.

'It should be pointed out', these scientists tell us, 'that ordinary photographic images cannot usually be converted to true three-dimensional reliefs. The more exposed – that is, the darker – sections of a photograph do not match those sections of the subject which were closer to the camera; the distance of the subject from the lens makes no difference to the intensity or definition of the resulting image. Only when an object, particularly a light, is very far away will the image it creates tend to vary in direct proportion to its distance from the camera. This is true of interplanetary and interstellar distances above all, and it is for this reason that the VP-8 was originally used by Air Force and other scientists as an aid in the work they did for the US space programme.'

Even through the soulless jargon of their trade the feelings that overcame them when they first saw that body and that face in three dimensions manages to creep through, as light might find its way through a heavy curtain. In the sequence featuring this experiment which David later filmed for *The Silent Witness*, that feeling is much more clearly expressed. Thus captured, it is brought to audiences directly. In the darkness, they too, the occasion the first for them as it once was for the scientists, can watch the slow materialisation of those lost dimensions, the assembly of features long vanished from the world, a fascinating extrapolation from what may be the only clue we have to the real appearance of Jesus.

What this work has proved is that "this three-dimensionality is a newly established, distinctive feature of the Shroud." But the experts then go on to examine the implications of this feature. First, they point out, whatever the process was that formed the image, it was uniform all over the body, since the only variations in intensity are caused by the distance from the body of the cloth. Second, the absence of gross distortions suggests that at the time "the Shroud was relatively flat". Third, if there were any factors other than variations in the cloth-body distances that might have altered the intensity of the image, they too must have acted uniformly all over the body. This in turn, they deduce, means that no random chemical or biological processes can have been at work on the Shroud during its history since these would have affected this overall uniformity. On the other hand, anything that would have affected the whole of the Shroud at once – they instance "full-length daylight expositions ... being boiled in oil, etc" – will have affected all of it equally without causing distortions in some part and not others.

One significant finding is their conclusion "that the image-forming process acted in the same manner on the bottom side of the body as on the top, because the characteristics of the bottom relief seem similar to those of the top relief", the logical implication of which is "that the process of image generation did not depend on pressure between the body and the cloth since, as just noted, equal contact intensities occurred on the top and bottom images where pressures at contact are greatly different. They also discount the possibility that chemicals in any way caused the image. These, they seem to feel, will have saturated certain areas of the cloth. Being in image terms very dark, these patches would have shown up on the three-dimensional projection as flat and level.

Jackson and Jumper also point up the importance of the fact that, no matter what the variation in intensity of the image, there is no variation in its resolution. This suggests that, however the 'information' was passed from the body to the cloth, the path it took was in all cases more or less perpendicular. This is supported by the fact that they could build up so relatively undistorted a three-dimensional picture of the image. In their own words, 'since a consistent three-dimensional image can be formed by perpendicular projection from the "zero intensity surface", which is equivalent to the cloth's surface in space, it follows that the image-forming process must have acted perpendicular to the Shroud, for otherwise an undistorted image of the surface of the body would be impossible to construct with the VP-8 Image Analyzer'. Of course, the perpendicular course that this mysterious process took underlines their earlier conclusion that the cloth itself was relatively flat. Had it not been, distortions not present in the transmission would have appeared in the reception – one may imagine the appearance of a photograph taken on a twisted film.

To see how their work might affect discussions over the Shroud's authenticity, they used their obliging VP-8 on reproductions of the Shroud replicas commissioned during the 1898 exhibition. These had already proved less than convincing when seen in negative; in three dimensions they displayed distortions of a pronounced nature. From this the scientists concluded, impeccably, 'Since two competent artists who had the Shroud to copy were unable to flawlessly produce a three-dimensional image from the Shroud, it would seem remote that some medieval artist could have achieved such an accomplishment with no Shroud available for reference.' Even if their English is not as elegant as their argument, it makes it clear that the genuineness of the Shroud has been substantially buttressed by their findings.

There were further discoveries to be made, however.

One of the most exciting was the discovery, on a three-dimensional projection of the face alone, that 'over each eye appeared objects resembling small buttons'. After discussing and rejecting a number of possibilities, they 'were left with but one conclusion – that the buttonlike features are what they seem to be, namely, *solid* objects resting upon the eyelids'. Their suggestion is that 'they may be some kind of coins'; if true, they add, they may have found 'a truly unique method of dating the image'. Indeed, they pass on information given them by Ian Wilson about a number of possible coins: 'In particular, a Lepton of Pontius Pilate coined in AD 30-31 seems to agree especially well. According to Wilson, a Lepton would probably be a likely candidate for Joseph of Arimathea, an orthodox Jew, to use since it was acceptable as a Temple offering.' Careful work with image enhancement equipment has shown up vague surface features on these objects, these probable coins, but they are not yet detailed enough to yield the potentially fascinating information they contain.

Dr Robinson, in his address, also referred to his three-dimensional projection of the head alone but focussed on a quite different aspect. Concerned to establish that the *suderion* was a jaw-band, wrapped around the head to keep the mouth closed (as the coins kept the eyes closed, he found 'a dark band immediately under the chin' that 'looks as if it is where the jaw-band has retracted a portion of the beard which would otherwise show up. The vertical dark strips on either side of the face, between the cheeks and the locks, otherwise so odd, could similarly be caused by the band holding back the intervening hair. The band would then continue up in front of the ears and under the hair which grows from the front part of the head, thus forcing it into prominence. It would then join over the crown of the head at the back, causing ... the "pinched" effect by which the head narrows to a point at the top.' The jaw-band, if it existed, Dr Robinson concludes, 'would be reflected on the Shroud, not only by where it

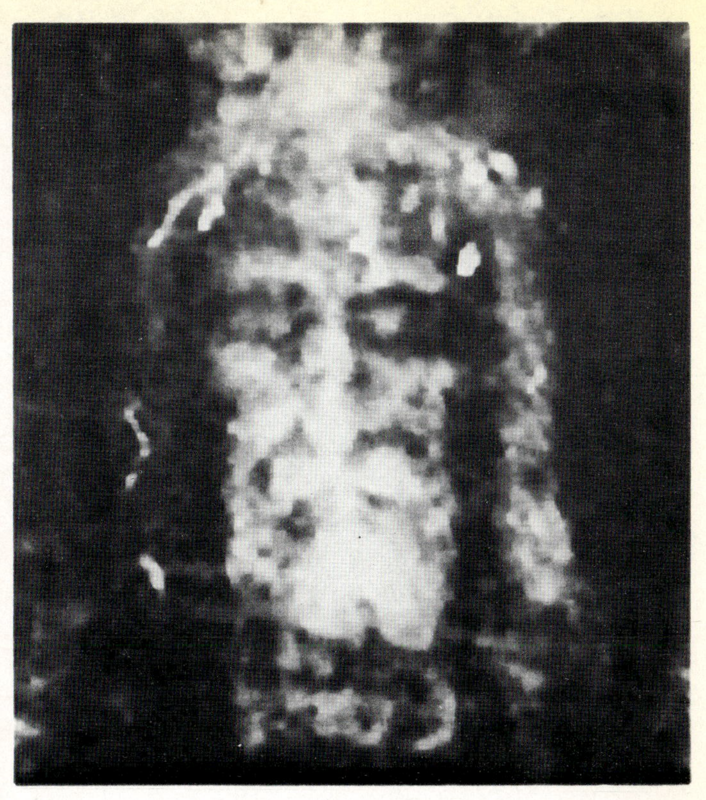

The image of the Shroud

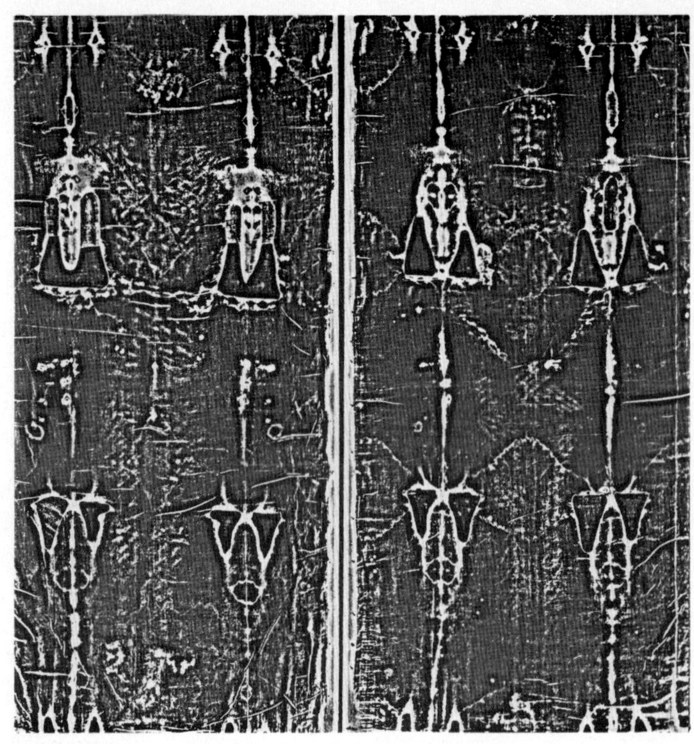

The Shroud full length, back and front

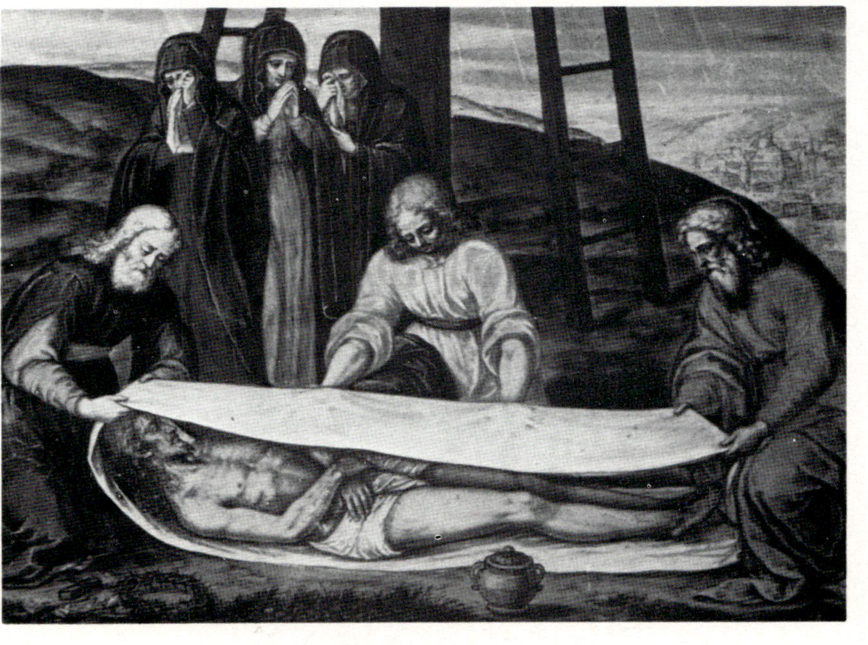

The Shroud: a traditional view

A reconstruction of the precise position according to the wounds on the Shroud that the body would have been in at the end of the crucifixion.

directly touches it, but still more by what it retracts and thus does not allow to show up.' Whether this is so or not, even a superficial examination makes plain. Supportive work to that done by Jackson, Jumper and Mottern was proposed by Lt. Thomas McCown, the first of several scientists who now put to the Conference their ideas on the next stage of Shroud research. Lt. McCown had made some preliminary measurements of cloth-body distances and suggested ways of establishing a more exact correlation between these and the variations of shade on the image. Having summarised what he calls the 'superb results from Dr Jackson's and Dr Jumper's experiment', he describes a possible further analysis of their three-dimensional projection. 'Precise knowledge of the functional relationship between cloth-body distance and image darkness will greatly aid the scientific determination of what process formed the Shroud image.'

Like Jackson and Jumper, McCown matched a prone man of the right physical proportions with the image on a replica of the Shroud (with their permission, he actually used the same replica). Using rays of light reflected in a mirror as his lines of calibration, McCown photographed the figure when covered and uncovered and carefully measured the resultant prints – he worked with enlargements or, better still, with the pictures projected on a wall. He would now be able to plot the cloth-body distances for any point on the Shroud with a care somewhat greater than his colleagues had attempted in the earlier experiment; using the capacity of a computer to store and to match mathematically encoded facts, he would then compare these distance measurements with the results of a survey for image-density which had already been undertaken. In the end, a computer could work out the precise mathematical function by which cloth-body distance and the darkness of the image were related. To test this, one might reverse the process: beginning with the image-density data, one would use the function already derived to turn these into cloth-body distances. 'Then the programme prints out similar data plots for a line across the Shroud at every 1/8 of an inch. These height printouts are then pasted to cardboard and the cardboard pieces are cut along the printouts ... If the cardboard pieces form a surface that looks like a body then the function that relates cloth-body distance to image darkness is consistently accurate throughout the image ... This function will demonstrate that the image was probably not hand-applied to the Shroud, and will aid scientists in their search for the process that made the image ...'

Lt. McCown's experiment has not yet of course taken place. His cardboard model, so painstakingly to be built up, has not yet applied to the work its final twist of corroboration. Yet it represents the kind of detailed and fertile thinking that has begun among those interested in Shroud research. If the experiment had been concluded and we did have some idea of that function, it might begin to narrow down the area in which the process that created the Shroud image should be looked for. It would provide a basis for further experimentation with possible methods (although not knowing the exact length of time it took to form the image might prove a substantial handicap), and a criterion for discarding those less in tune with the essential mathematics.

Other scientists offered suggestions for work that should be put in hand. Capt. Joseph Accetta, of the U.S. Air Force Weapons Laboratory, for example, outlined an X-ray flourescence analysis by means of which trace elements in the chemistry of the Shroud might be identified – most notably, the presence or absence of blood might be once and for all determined. He also suggested tests by infrared thermography, a technique measuring the distinctive emissions in the infra-red region of the spectrum, by means of which the surface properties of the Shroud and its image might be determined and areas in which chemical changes have taken or are taking place might be defined. The variation in infra-red emission as between one point and another on the Shroud might well, he feels, give us new information on 'the chemical composition of the image-forming material' – a problem which has so far baffled all analysis.

Dr Walter McCrone, a scientist with his own consultancy firm in Chicago, proposed various experiments which might help to authenticate the Shroud. One, frequently mentioned even by laymen, is by the now well-established carbon dating techniques. The problem in the past has been that too large a section of the Shroud would have had to be burned to make such a method suitable for so precious a relic. The latest techniques, however, as Dr McCrone points out, far from requiring the piece of material forty centimeters square necessary in 1950, would use an area of only two square centimeters. (He does not refer to other objections to this technique, however, notably the fact that during its exhibition and the viscissitudes of his history, the Shroud will have become so contaminated that any carbon dating will be too imprecise to be useful; and that in any case such a dating, even at its best, lacks the kind of precision essential in the matter of the Shroud, for which, unlike a piece of Hittite earthenware or an Etruscan mural, a range of even a few decades in the result would render it almost useless).

Dr McCrone went on to suggest that the stains on the Shroud, and the composition of the image itself, should be examined by the ion microscope. 'It identifies all elements and even organic compounds. It is able to identify samples invisible even with the light microscope. It detects, on one tiny spot on one of my scalp hairs, for example, more than 30 trace elements attesting to the fact that such a hair can only have come from my head ... Only three years ago such analyses were impossible ...' He expressed his confidence 'that the results will answer the question of blood and give us new and useful, hopefully definitive, information on the image'.

Before he ended his paper, Dr McCrone had a plethora of techniques to offer, any one of which might extend the limits of knowledge about the Shroud: tests of the blood stains with various catalysts; analysis of all the dust on the Shroud, collected with a 'micro vacuum cleaner'; reflecting X-ray flourescence and infra-red thermography, as already proposed, to isolate the elements present and, in the case of the latter, possibly to increase the contrast on the image itself; X-ray radiography and photography at different wavelengths from infra-red to ultra-violet; micro Raman, a method of identifying minute quantities of compounds both organic and inorganic, capable of determining the presence of blood, and even of aloes or spices, should these exist in the smallest significant amount; and every variety of microscopy.

Dr Ray Rodgers, an archaeologist with the advantage of having been trained as a physical chemist, addressed himself to the problem of testing for the presence or absence of inorganic pigments in the image (the lack of reaction to the heat of the 1538 fire having eliminated the possibility of its having been painted in organic colours). He advocates multiple X-ray fluorescence as the technique best able to deal with this, considering it 'the most important non-destructive test that can be run during the 1978 viewing'. Like Dr McCrone, he proposes the use of the ion microprobe to discover if long-lasting molecular remnants may be discerned in areas that seem to be bloodstained. In his opinion the evidence suggests 'rapid heating as the cause of the image. An image originally formed by the thermal discolouration of the cloth would not change colour or density significantly with any additional heating that did not discolour the surrounding cloth. If X-ray fluorescence does not identify any pigment on the cloth and no thermally stable organic pigment can be suggested, this appears to be the only hypothesis left.' Electron spectroscopy for chemical analysis or reflectance spectrometry, using a cloth especially marked by heat for comparison would, he feels, help to establish this even further: 'It may not be possible to prove conclusively that the image is the result of thermal degradation of the cloth, but a very strong circumstantial case could be made'.

The rest of the scientific papers concerned the kinds of photographs that might be taken of the Shroud and the kinds of experimental uses to which they might be put. The techniques for image enhancement are many, and that they can be marvellously effective is clear from the work already done, not only by Dr Jackson and Dr Jumper but also, alone or in association with some of the others, by Don Devan of Information Science and by Jean Lorre and Donald Lynn of the Jet Propulsion Laboratory, as well as by Donald Janney of the Los Alamos Laboratory. Work of this sort came into existence during the Second World War, when photographs taken during aerial reconnaissance had to be assessed quickly and with the highest accuracy. Not only greater magnifications but new kinds of magnification, new kinds of examination under new kinds of light, new sorts of projections made by new applications of mathematics – these were the techniques that then had their first tentative beginnings.

After the war ended, such recently developed methods found a new outlet in the aerial surveys by which vast areas of the globe were accurately mapped for the first time. Other uses began to be developed as an ancillary element in optical astronomy. Computers, with their capacity to store and draw on information, and adapted to display their results on a television screen, were brought in to add their speed and precision to the process. Then came President Kennedy's determined campaign to put a man on the moon, the vastly accelerated space programme, the need to discover from the sources available every iota of information about the far reaches of space. Astrophysics demanded a finer and finer resolution, not only in the observations astronomers made but also in the analyses of these observations. Cosmology became one of the great speculative sciences of the day, and by various means mankind became aware of a new variety of phenomena in the deep reaches of space. Thus stimulated, the art of image-enhancement began its swift advance. It is now at the very frontiers of computer technology, incorporating every development almost as soon as it occurs. It is the awe-inspiring battery of its machineries and techniques that, in addition to all the methods of direct investigation, Dr Jackson, Dr Jumper and their colleagues hope will provide in the very near future some solutions to the abiding enigmas of the Shroud.

At the Albuquerque Conference, the battle lines were drawn up, the plans for an advance were laid; perhaps even the signal was given for that advance to begin. The experiments so far conducted have left the Shroud as strange and unyielding a mystery as it ever was. For scientists, that fact offers a challenge to the central preoccupation of their lives. Mysteries there may be in the metaphysical sphere, but the physical world is theirs. Nothing, they instinctively feel, may withstand them there. Yet the Holy Shroud of Turin has, so far, withstood their efforts to understand it and to analyse and anatomise the process that created it and the elements it contains. The implication lying behind what most of them said at Albuquerque was that this state of affairs could not be tolerated, that it could not be allowed to go on much longer.

As for David Rolfe, this overwhelming scientific certainty helped to confirm him in his own convictions. Nothing, he was determined, should divert him from his intention to base *The Silent Witness* on cool logic and a considered objectivity. Whatever his own feelings or the pressures others might bring to bear, his film would be a document, not a sermon. Anything else would be a betrayal of the integrity displayed by so many of the researchers who had demonstrated the results of their work and their hopes for the future during the Albuquerque Conference.

CHAPTER EIGHT

As Roger Connolly walked along the little Soho lane, he began to wonder what sort of film company he was trying to join. At intervals, slightly seedy restaurants dispensed the foods of distant lands. Bored Indian faces peered through the spattered windows of a hire-car office. On the small corner cinema garish posters in incomprehensible Chinese advertised the violent attractions of Hong Kong epics. At some windows glistened the patient smiles of knowing girls; at others, the jowly faces of Greek tailors. Dusty neon lights waited for nightfall to announce the debatable attractions of cellar clubs. Meard Street. Connolly glanced dubiously up and down its length; even the hundred yards of its grimly glamorous course looked crooked.

David, for his part, trying to engage a production manager, was faced with a choice of strangers, experienced men who had answered his advertisement. All of them had more or less equally convincing credentials. Roger Connolly, for example, had worked on television documentaries, on a series or two, on a handful of films. There was no reason to take him on, no reason not to, no reason not to choose any one of the other applicants. It was the same unexpected factor that resolved both their doubts – a picture of the Shroud. Roger, seeing it on the wall of David's office, nodded at it. 'That's the Holy Shroud of Turin, isn't it?'

Surprised, David said it was. Roger smiled. 'I've just been reading a book about it.' Only that day he had finished Father Rinaldi's *The Man in the Shroud*, without the slightest idea that his approaching interview concerned a film on the subject. The coincidence both allayed Roger's suspicions of the Meard Street address and decided David's choice of production manager. From now on there was another pair of shoulders on which David could heap much of the detailed work still necessary. This included the hiring of most of the crew. The only choices he himself made concerned the cameramen.

Behram Manocheri is an Iranian, large, heavily moustached, intense and ferociously meticulous in his work. He was also trained at the London Film School; by the time that David was a student there, he had become one of its lecturers in cinematography. From the beginning David wanted Behram's still-developing talent, for which he has immense respect, to be employed on *The Silent Witness*. Now at last, with his project so well under way, he was able to approach the Iranian with real proposals. Happily, Bahram agreed to join the unit.

That left one crucial question – should David himself direct the film? That he was so close to it, and had been close to it for so long, was clearly both an advantage and a handicap. His ideas on it could well have hardened into inflexibility during the two years that had already passed. The excitement that comes from a confrontation with the new had, he felt, long ago died down. On the other hand, he knew every turn of the film's argument and its every location; he had seen each sequence develop and had supervised the development of most of them. Yet he felt that, on the whole, a fresh eye was likely to give the final version an energy and an attack which might be lacking if he were to be the director.

He began to interview possible candidates. To his surprise he seemed unable to find anyone with the right credentials who was also prepared to take the subject seriously. For almost all of them, the Shroud was a sort of peepshow triviality, a film about which would have to be an exposé, a satire or a patronising dismissal. A few showed signs of being ready to veer in the other direction and make a reverential sermon on celluloid. Neither was what David was looking for: a cool but respectful appraisal of the possible history and the actual facts. The young director he finally chose, although a man with experience of both film and television documentaries – so far only as first assistant director – recommended himself as much by the thoughtful seriousness of his attitude as by his talents as a film-maker. His only stipulation was that he should bring his own cameraman with him; when David pointed out that, with Bahram already chosen, this was impossible, he accepted the situation with rather less good grace than was immediately apparent. It was a difference that, hardly noticed by David at the time, would in due course have its consequences.

Henry Lincoln, meanwhile, had been working on a final version of the script. It was this that would decide whether that bell sounded for the final lap or whether Harry John cut the race short. The time for the Albuquerque Conference was drawing closer; it was there that the last decisions would be taken. Impatiently, David waited for Lincoln to do his work.

He had also included a new face among those who would be appearing in the film. This was the Rt Rev. Dr John Robinson, now Master of Trinity College, Cambridge, but previously Anglican Bishop of Woolwich. It was another clergyman, the Rev. David Sox, an American teaching in London whose long interest in the Shroud has been as a Church historian rather than a scientist, who first suggested Dr Robinson as a participant. During his episcopal years Dr Robinson had written, among other books, *Honest to God*, that popular summary of radical Protestant theology which, bringing the subject within reach of the mass-circulation press, had also brought controversy down upon his head.

David felt surprised that so cool and sceptical a churchman, one who during the cannonading of his critics had even been called an atheist, should have displayed public interest in so awe-inspiring a relic. But Dr Robinson's testimony might provide David's film with a cool Protestant balance for the Catholic impetuosity of

Monsignor Ricci. He travelled to Cambridge and found Dr Robinson co-operative and manifestly fascinated by the Shroud. Indeed, he was curious to hear news of all the latest research being done in the United States, notably the work of Jackson and Jumper at Colorado Springs; their three-dimensional reconstructions of the Shroud image had recently emphasised the chin-band on which he himself was then writing a paper. He readily agreed to take part in *The Silent Witness*, a participation reinforced by his accepting David's invitation to fly him to the Albuquerque Conference.

That pregnant meeting with Harry John was also to take place at Albuquerque, far more important for David and *The Silent Witness* than any conference. Henry Lincoln's script arrived, incorporating Ian Wilson's work and scenes written by David himself, the whole an end-product of months of thought, of debate, of notes passed to and fro, of argument and disagreement, of co-operation, of advice offered and taken, of tiny defeats and even tinier triumphs. For a while Wilson was to disagree with the way it had turned out, threatening to halt the project or somehow remove himself, but that was the result of the intensity at which they were all for the moment living. They were too close to the crucial decisions now, and the tension sometimes showed in their behaviour.

New Mexico, therefore, in early spring: a thin air and a thin sunshine crackling with the last sharpness of winter – before David left, it was to snow once more, a flurry left over from the icy months just past. The meeting place was a conference room in their hotel, itself a consciously noble building modelled on the high colonial style but executed in moulded-plaster detail. Yet the columned portico impressed, and the manner of building was as profoundly rooted in the culture as was the choice of architecture.

Albuquerque had been selected because it was central to the scientists who worked in the clean new industries and military bases of the developing South-West and West. As the conference delegates gathered, however, one could see among the short-haired, crisp-suited technocrats and the collared clergymen, clusters of quite different men: long-haired, bearded, sandalled, in worn jeans and faded denim shirts. At first, these caused consternation. Had they really been invited? People asked each other who they were – and found that the answer was The Brotherhood of Christ. This was a small group which had, like so many in the modern United States, opted for a simpler life than the cities provided. They had their headquarters in the hills near Albuquerque and there attempted to live a life modelled on that of Jesus and his precepts, running a hostel that offered food and a bed to anyone who needed and asked for them. Having heard of this conference so near them, they had decided to attend, soon discovering – not at all against their first expectations – that everyone looked at them somewhat askance. It quickly became clear, however, that there was a generosity and a pertinance to their contributions which enforced a general respect; by the end of the two-day meeting, several of them had become very friendly with delegates of a more regular background – whose academic credentials, incidentally, they could often match. They gave to the whole conference not only an unscheduled breadth of approach and a touch of romanticism but also a curious modernity without which it would have been diminished.

Early on, David himself was asked to speak. He stood up to do so with a little trepidation. Harry John, as yet not finally committed, Ian Wilson, for the moment blankly at odds with him, and Monsignor Ricci, anxious to wrest from him control in the venture, were all among the eighty or so people waiting to hear him. He could feel like tiny pinpricks the hard brightness of their stares as he waited by the rostrum. He was not helped by the fact that, just after having been introduced – 'David Rolfe, of Screenpro Films, from London, England' – and before he could say a word, some jinxed alarm clock suddenly blared out, intended to warn to long-winded speakers. 'I see my reputation has preceded me!' he murmured drily, turning the laugh.

He picked his way carefully through his speech; under each phrase lurked a potential land-mine primed to blow up his venture: his meeting with Harry John was still a day away. He was at the conference, he said, only as 'a fascinated observer'. Other speakers had spoken of the need to make more widely available evidence about the Shroud, 'and that is the purpose of this film – to encapsulate the evidence, particularly the new evidence, for the authenticity of the Shroud ... to present this new evidence to an audience who will I hope approach it very sceptically, not at all committed to the idea that the Shroud could be genuine'. The Shroud was in itself 'a natural detective story'; his main objective was in no sense religious – 'I certainly won't try and set out to preach'. He pointed out that script approval was by the terms of the contract to be based only on scientific and objective grounds, 'a testimony to the attitude taken by the Holy Shroud Guild'. Eighty per cent of the film's proceeds, he told his largely scientific audience, would be made available for research into and dissemination of knowledge about the Shroud. He ended by mentioning a recent, somewhat catchpenny film about Noah's Ark: 'It's superficial similarities to this project are obvious, but its scholastic nature can only be described as spurious'. *The Silent Witness* would, he hoped, create the same kind of interest but do something the other film did not, 'and that is retain a very firm and well authenticated scholastic and objective background'.

Having thus run up his own colours and, in effect, laid down once again both the terms on which he was making the film and his sense of obligation for being allowed to do so, he settled back to enjoy the conference itself, and to learn from it whatever might be useful. He did not really expect argument or opposition, although Harry John's doubts about the film or about him as its producer might yet prove a barrier too high for him to leap over. That, however, was something that he would discover only during the meeting scheduled for the next day. When he went to bed that night, he was so tense that, for a long time, he could not sleep – and then, as is happily often the case, he fell asleep, even as he wondered if he would ever sleep again.

At three in the morning, the telephone dragged him from ease. His eyes still closed, his head feeling full of straw, he heard as though in a dream the soft voice in the receiver of Elizabeth Maria Patizzi, Monsignor Ricci's assistant. It would be best if his film followed the Vatican line, the voice was telling him; he had better do what Vatican servants asked him to do. If he did not, there might be no film. Had he reckoned with that? If he really wanted the film made, he had better agree to the conditions that had already been demanded. He knew what to do – she was sure that during the next morning's meeting he would do it. Too tired to argue, David muttered, 'Don't threaten me!' The line went dead.

The trial of his nerves was not yet over, however. When the next morning he met Father Otterbein at breakfast, he was alarmed to see how strained and severe his face was.

'What's the matter, Father?' he asked anxiously.

The president of the Holy Shroud Guild made a small grimace. 'I've had a wire', he said. 'From Hollywood.'

David stared. 'Hollywood!' Were they about to be taken over by Warner Brothers?

Otterbein said, 'They're going to make a film about the Shroud!' Waves of nausea began to shake David; he was afraid that he might fall down. He remembers to this day the feeling of weakness, of physical helplessness, that kept him silent and immobile. After all he had gone through, after the two years of struggle, was he about to lose his film? Father Otterbein was meanwhile telling him that for years the Guild had been trying to persuade Hollywood to make a motion picture on the subject; now, without warning they had apparently agreed.

The key word, however, is 'apparently'. In retrospect,

David is convinced that this was a deliberate attempt to wreck the film, if not by one of the individuals already involved then by someone who had discovered that everything concerning the finances had not yet been entirely settled. Certainly there has been no word of such an epic since, nor the slightest confirming hint that it was contemplated. Nor was it ever absolutely clear to David who in Hollywood had been seized at eight o'clock that morning with an urgency sufficient to drive them hot-foot to the telephone.

It was now that Father Otterbein's coolness and practicality came into its own. It was his principle to prefer a bird in the hand to even the most brightly coloured flock in some nearby bush – particularly when that bush derived from the eccentric shrubberies of Hollywood. His dealings with film people over the years had taught him how ephemeral their plans were, and how brittle their promises; he was a priest who had learned his way about that world. He stood firm, therefore: *The Silent Witness* was the project in hand and *The Silent Witness* was the project he would support. With an effort David, over his orange juice and scrambled eggs, built around the new threat a *cordon sanitaire* of enforced indifference. Since he could do nothing about Hollywood, his only alternative was to ignore it. Once again he began mentally to prepare himself for the conference ahead.

It was to be held in Harry John's hotel suite. Dr Gallagher would be there, of course, and Father Rinaldi, Father Otterbein – and Monsignor Ricci, who to aid him would have, naturally enough, the multilingual Elizabeth Maria Patizzi. As David walked towards that fateful door, he saw her ahead of him, slowing, turning her head, watching him. For a moment he could hear again her low voice murmuring demands in his ear, as it had over the telephone only six hours earlier. She half-smiled, an enigmatic grimace, came closer and gently took his arm.

'You know Harry John listens to every word Monsignor Ricci says, don't you?' she said. 'You know that. Yes. So are you going to do ... what is best for the Shroud?' She gave the final phrase a special significance, as if to imply that 'best for the Shroud' was synonymous with 'what Monsignor Ricci wants'. David, however, carefully accepted only the surface meaning, with which he could deal with the problem. He looked at her, open-eyed.

'Yes', he said. 'Of course.'

For a fraction of a second they faced each other expressionlessly and in silence. What had they actually said? What might each read into these phrases. Then, with a tiny smile, a tinier shrug, Elizabeth turned away. They went into Harry John's rooms.

David was tense, nervously expectant and prepared for crucial decisions. Impatiently he sat through the jovial preliminaries, the directionless discussions, the weak jokes and misapplied seriousness which always attend such meetings. At last the moment arrived for the script, that profoundly significant wad of paper, to become the focus of debate. A handful of responses, affirmative or negative, were about to decide the present shape of his life.

Father Rinaldi was delighted with the script; it was what he had hoped and expected. An affirmative. Father Otterbein, with a down-to-earth enthusiasm, agreed. An affirmative. Monsignor Ricci was more hesitant. The script was very good, of course, yet there should be a change or two, a shift of emphasis here or there – on which he would naturally be glad to give guidance. Nevertheless, by and large, on the whole ... Grudgingly then, an affirmative. All eyes now on Harry John, perhaps the only one there whose agreement was absolutely essential, the man with his hands on the necessary gold. He fiddled with the paper in front of him, looking down at the floor.

He said, 'I'm going to reserve judgement'.

David stared at him. What did that mean? Had Harry John read the script and disliked it? Had he read it and been unable to decide whether he liked it. Had Monsignor Ricci persuaded him to hold back judgement? Or had he not read it at all? David licked his lips, cleared his throat.

'When can we expect a decision?' he asked.

'I can't say at this time.' Portentously, Harry John nodded his heavy head.

David said, 'All right. I have to go to California to talk to some distribution people there. Can I come and see you in Milwaukee on my way back?'

'That'd be great, David. Great.' Harry John smiled. He seemed to have no idea of the rack on which he had left David and the others. Perhaps, though, he did relish protracting a decision which, once made, would see all control over the venture finally pass from him. He was still smiling amiably, with the cultivated unconcern of the very rich, when David left the room, and perhaps even the following day when, the conference itself over, the various delegates flew off in their many directions – David himself westward to California.

It was only a few days and a handful of indecisive business meetings later that David again found himself face-to-face with Harry John. This time the two men were alone in the millionaire's office. The atmosphere was peaceful, but David felt his muscles tense as the moment arrived for the decision to be given. Harry John flicked the pages of the script. Like a client at an emperor's court, David watched the hand that held his fate.

'I've read the script', Harry John said. He offered the remark as though in itself it constituted significant news. David nodded. Harry John said, portentously, 'David, I want to tell you something'. In the pause that followed, David nodded, licked his lips – months of work and thousands of dollars had built towards this instant. Harry John looked up, tapped the paper softly with his index finger.

'On Page 75 here – did you know you'd spelled 'messenger' wrong?'

For a speechless second David stared at him. Which of them had gone insane? Then he collected himself. 'No!' he exclaimed, feigning the horror that seemed called for.

'Yep! Spelled it wrong. I noticed that.'

David bent down hastily flicking pages. 'My God!' he babbled. 'You're right! Well, I'll get that altered. I'll tell them to correct that right away. I'm grateful you found it.'

Harry John leaned back, smiling. He had made his criticism, effected his intervention – and, in the process, shot his bolt. He had nothing else to say. Spelling apart, it seemed, the script was excellent. David had been given the final approval that he needed. The last-lap bell had sounded. If he could keep his feet until the tape, he might yet run out the winner. In order to make more certain of this, however, he needed one more assurance from Harry John. Taking his courage in both hands, he broached quite directly the whole subject of Monsignor Ricci. He was prepared, he said, to work with Monsignor Ricci, to listen to advice from him, to be deferential and respectful – but he was not prepared to hand over the slightest element of authority or the tiniest fraction of directorial responsibility. He waited for argument, but in castigating his spelling Harry John had exhausted all tendency to criticise.

'That's all right', he said comfortingly. 'That's OK, David.'

David had his film – and, more than that, he had made sure it would remain his film. As he walked down the carpetted corridors towards the guarded entrance of the building, his face was stretched in a smile that owed nothing whatever to diplomatic necessity.

In Britain, Roger Connolly was well advanced in his gathering of a crew, selecting people who had already had some Middle Eastern experience. David suggested as assistant cameraman Paul Turtle, a contemporary and friend of his at the London Film School. Meanwhile, the director was busily making his own preliminary plans. David's life, by contrast with what had gone before, was suddenly all ease and comfort. The final version of his script had been approved; he had beaten off Monsignor

Ricci, while Ian Wilson, having looked more deeply into the actual politics of the film, was returning to his earlier understanding friendliness. So far, the final lap was proving the most painless of them all.

It was necessary for both production manager and director to see at first hand what problems they would face when filming began. David arranged to accompany the two of them on a second reconnaissance of the terrain. In the late spring of 1977, they flew off on the first leg of their trip to Istanbul, which David now found familiar with its mixture of the exotic, the tumbledown and the second-rate modern. Without incident they wandered through their chosen locations, but David was conscious of a new coldness in the general atmosphere. There had been political changes in the country, a right-wing government had taken power, and everywhere the show of force with which it was trying to regularise its position was unpleasantly obvious. There were more uniforms in evidence, more weapons. Among the people there was, not unexpectedly, more resentment. It was a situation that would, in time, have some repercussions on their own plans. Now, however, with Samim to guide them, they simply ignored an authoritarianism which they felt had nothing to do with them.

So clearly did David have the city of Urfa in his memory that the new reality he actually found seemed for a while unreal. What he had thought of as a near-desert had been overtaken by the Anatolian spring. Everywhere was fertility, green groves, fields heavy with crops, trees bowed with fruit. The market overflowed with plums and apples, maize and melons. For the first time David realised how rich this land was – it was indeed that Mesopotamia which had supported the wealth of the Ziggurat-dominated settlements of Ur, Nineveh and Babylon, which echo with an undiminished power down the years.

If his historical sense was stimulated, however, he could not deny that so much fertility threatened his plans. How was he going to film near Urfa as Max Frei meant to be busy in the wilderness of Judaea? In the winter it had been possible, but they would not be filming in winter; if, when they did, it looked as it was looking now, there was no chance that they could cobble together a sufficiently cunning sequence. He began to search for some spot that might, a little later in the year, prove suitable, and did indeed find one. When the time came, however, it turned out to be useless.

Their stay was more comfortable this time, partly because the staff of the city's one acceptable hotel recognised him. Not many people travel to Urfa, and of this select group very few come twice. The hotel staff felt honoured, therefore, and treated him like a friend. For his part, David on this visit made a discovery that contributed a great deal to his general satisfaction – he found where the key to the WC was kept! Upon such minute particulars turns the welfare of pioneers.

One task to which they applied themselves was the discovery of a hand-loom weaver. It was by a craftsman of this kind that the Shroud had been woven, and the film needed to show how it had been done. For a long time they searched without success – they spoke no Turkish, Samim was not with them, and gestures count little towards describing something as complex as a loom. Looking back, David recognises how patronising was their conviction that they would find such craftsmen in great numbers. What they actually found were modern factories turning out textiles by the mile. It was at one of these, however, that they were given the directions they had been hoping for from the beginning.

The man they reached was, they eventually discovered, one of only three hand-loom weavers left in the region. Nevertheless, he was exactly what they had been looking for. In his workroom, gnarled wooden frames stood under an ancient, pitted ceiling and absorbed craftsmen turned out their cloth with the quiet clattering that had resounded through the Middle East for hundreds upon hundreds of years. Every corner of the room was taken up with the machines. Outside, in a little courtyard, hens huddled in the dust, making their languorous midday croaking. Muffled women hurried by, bent on household tasks. Despite linguistic barriers, David was able to establish from the watchful owner, a sly-eyed old man with a seamed face, dressed in the traditional baggy trousers of the country, that when the film crew returned, they would be able to shoot among his looms the sequence they wanted.

Time was beginning to run against them. Far to the west Monsignor Ricci in his Rome offices awaited a meeting. Setting off from ancient Edessa, David reflected that in Roman terms he was setting off on a journey from the very edge of the empire to its centre. Had he been an imperial legate, however, he would have spent a week or more on the road, while as it was he had just this one day. On the first stage, he must have wished he had been restricted to the comparative comfort of a chariot. His taxi-driver, whirling along the loose-surfaced road to Gaziente, thrust himself so closely under the tail-boards of speeding trucks and lorries that, a few miles out of Urfa, the windscreen was shattered by flying stones. Learning no lessons from this he forced his terrified passengers to take cover flat on their seats as, unhampered, pebbles, granite chips and jagged lumps of rock flung an endless assault down the length of the car. It was, David insists, the only time he has seen a stone fly in the front of a car with a velocity sufficient to crack the rear window. They were delighted to begin with unpunctured skin the next stage of their journey, which was the flight to Ankara and, a little later, Istanbul.

There David separated from the other two, leaving them to settle final arrangements for the filming with Samim. He flew on to his talks with Monsignor Ricci and his assistant. Again the pleasant luxury of office and apartment, again the visible friendliness, the evident hospitality – and again, the underlying struggle. By now, David knew very clearly what problems and what advantages Monsignor Ricci represented. He had already planned, at least in part, the sequence in which the clergyman would appear, his observations on the wounds carried by the man in the Shroud image intercut with Dr Bucklin's scientific descriptions. Monsignor Ricci, however, was a little disturbed at the role he was to play: 'I do not want to be the altar-boy to Dr Bucklin's cardinal'. Smiling, he asked for reassurance and, smiling, David gave it to him. Looking back, he thinks with a faint feeling of guilt that he may have given Monsignor Ricci a slightly inflated impression of the part he was to play. Directors, though, can offer those who take part in their films no certainties. The participants perform as they are asked and take their pay or credit, but how what they do is used depends on the slow dramas, the experiments and discoveries of the cutting-room. It is there that films are shaped and only at that stage that binding decisions can be taken. Many an actor has found his career made or marred not before the turning cameras but under the incisive scissors of an editor.

By the time David's colleagues joined him from Istanbul, therefore, Monsignor Ricci felt a renewed confidence in the project and in his own involvement with it. This was reinforced by the ease with which his other requests – that his lecture-room and study should be featured – were agreed to. They turned out to be lively locations and give a certain vividness to parts of the film that otherwise might have seemed visually without much interest. So great was Monsignor Ricci's good humour that he asked David to stay behind an extra day when the moment for departure arrived. While the other two travelled on to Turin, therefore, David took a jaunt into the Italian summer with this now-friendly priest.

They travelled some hundred kilometers north of Rome to the monastery where, as a thirty-year-old priest, Monsignor Ricci had picked up Barbet's book and first become fascinated by the Holy Shroud of Turin. They walked through gardens drowsy with the scents of a hundred flowers, by the gentle sweep of branches in the breeze, by the weight of sea and mountain on either side. The throbbing notes of distant plainsong floated softly on sunlight, the endless chanting which for two thousand years has been the sound of the Church's complex machinery of worship signalling humanity's awe of the divine. Tears stood in Monsignor Ricci's eyes as he looked about him. Was it the grandeur of the centuries or the memorials of his youth that made him sob? Elizabeth nudged David. 'See how he is moved!' she murmured. 'See how it affects him!' The remark falsified the emotion, drained the scene of its simplicity. Was Monsignor Ricci feeling what he seemed to, or was he demonstrating the feeling that he ought to? 'She subtitled all his actions', David says. 'So one came to doubt their genuineness.'

Certainly there was some motive in Monsignor Ricci's suggesting this outing – he hinted that, if *The Silent Witness* proved successful, he could persuade Harry John to sponsor a film about his own work on the Shroud and how he had come to develop his ideas.

Catching a train at Padua, David arrived in Turin at one o'clock in the morning. The next day, he could relax in the less demanding company of Don Coreo as always pleased to see him and happy to be undemandingly co-operative. The municipal authorities, responsible for the Chapel of the Shroud, and the cathedral authorities, to whose building the chapel is attached, had to approve David's proposed filming, but they were pleased to give what assistance they could. David was promised the actual hangings with which the cathedral had been decorated during the 1898 exhibition of the Shroud. It was then that Secondo Pia had taken his famous photographs, an event that David wanted to reproduce for the film. 'If you bring a replica of the Shroud, we can exhibit it in the very same frame as on the evening when Pia set up his camera' – official enthusiasm was running almost as high as his own.

It was in the highest spirits, therefore, that the three

men, the free-ranging advance guards of the production, drove over the St Gothard and down into Switzerland. In Zurich, Max Frei awaited their visit – although at the precise moment when they tried to make contact with him, he proved to be unavailable. The reason only confirmed his all-round reliability: he was at a board meeting of one of Zurich's many notable financial institutions. This gnome-like preoccupation emphasised the solidity of his reputation and the respectability of his background. Had there been the slightest doubt about his evidence, this close connection with finance must surely have allayed it.

They were, nevertheless, to suffer disappointment in Zurich. They had expected Max Frei's house to offer them a background which would make instantly clear the scientific standing of the criminologist. A rack of test-tubes, perhaps, a conveniently placed microscope, a work-bench, a Bunsen burner or two, the gleam of flasks, pipettes, retorts. Instead they found a perfectly ordinary, pleasantly comfortable, tidy middle-class house. A man might be at ease there, but as the background for a filmed interview with a scientist it lacked the relevance of a laboratory. Audiences need instant signals, indications of where they are and who it is that they are listening to. A man in a white coat, surrounded by the complex paraphernalia of obscure experimentation, hardly needs to be introduced – we have learned to hang upon the lips of such oracles. The same man relaxing in an armchair in his living-room needs to have his credentials laid out with some emphasis before we pay him the same attention. David therefore determined to construct a background for Max Frei. The money he saved by not filming in Zurich could be spent in making the necessary arrangements in London. And, with their reconnaissance successfully completed, it was to London that the three men now returned, to lay their final plans and make whatever dispositions were still necessary before filming could begin.

David now put in hand something the need for which had become clearly apparent during the visit to Turin – a replica of the Shroud. They had to have a cloth they could film, and with the real Shroud so carefully locked away, they were faced with a task easy to define but difficult to accomplish. And David knew the man who would be able to achieve it.

John Weston is broad-shouldered, clear-eyed, relaxed; a loner, an individualist, almost by definition self-taught; a man who seems, nevertheless, to have found precisely his right niche. He is a designer who first worked with David Rolfe on the title sequences for *The Great Gatsby* and has often done so since. David says of him, 'He's amazingly skilful and imaginative when faced with unusual situations' – and making a replica of the Holy Shroud of Turin was certainly unusual.

Leo Vala, known for devising a technique to make three-dimensional figures from photographs, who had long been interested in the Shroud, had already attempted to make a replica by printing the image on cloth. Unfortunately, the material necessary was much too heavy to be easily handled, and when it was folded the picture on it creased so deeply that it became unusable. It was when he realised how difficult it was going to be to produce the kind of replica he needed that David turned to John Weston. That was the person he thought of whenever a design problem threatened to prove insuperable.

John for his part was under no illusion about how difficult it was going to be – if he had been, it would not have been for long. At first, he too thought that a replica image might be expertly printed and asked one of the biggest wallpaper manufacturers in the country whether they might do it. The Shroud was fourteen feet long and only a little over three-and-a-half feet wide, proportions very similar to those of a strip of wallpaper. The manufacturers, however, were not optimistic. The marvellously fine gradations of shading and colour would be very difficult to reproduce, it would take a long time to make the plates, even if it could be done, and for the creation of a single object the cost would be prohibitive. The subtlety of the image necessitated several printings and there was no guarantee that a cloth of the light weight David had specified would not move during the process. That, of course, would alter the register of the plates and blur the image. It would no longer be exactly what was on the Shroud but a second-rate version of it. For a whole afternoon, John telephoned printers of every technical persuasion, but all of them said much the same: it would be a difficult and very expensive operation.

Then John thought that perhaps he could turn a piece of cloth into a sort of photographic base. By dipping it in emulsion and exposing it to a picture of the Shroud, he would be able to take a photograph directly on to it. The size of the Shroud, however, made this an impossible venture. Then he thought that perhaps the special printers who prepare street-wide banners might have a solution, but they did not work with such subtleties as the Shroud displayed.

Finally he had a moment of muted triumph. He had brought a piece of cheesecloth from his wife's dress shop. In his studio, desperate, he dipped it in a cup of cold tea. As the pale brown stain slowly spread on the soft cloth, he saw that it was almost precisely the right strength and colour. Could he make the Shroud image of cold tea? He thought not – but it gave him a clue about what he would need: some sort of water-based colour that would spread in the same way.

How was he to apply it? He considered using an air-brush but finally rejected the idea. It would give a smooth, even texture, but it was not positive enough for the detail, nor could it be removed if one made a mistake. In fourteen feet of work, he thought ruefully, there were bound to be mistakes. With a deep sigh he arrived at the only remaining solution – the whole picture would have to be done bit by bit, an inch at a time, by hand with a brush.

He took a close-up of one of the burn marks, a black-and-white, life-sized version of the original. Under this he laid tracing paper, and beneath that a piece of the cheesecloth. Slowly, he traced the irregular lozenge of the mark, then removed the paper. There it lay, pale red upon the cloth. He mixed up two or three dabs of ochre gouaches until he had a colour that resembled the original cold tea. With a slim brush, he began to apply this to the cheesecloth. The surface proved too dry, however, and the colour sat on it unevently. Carefully, he dampened the cloth, then laid down paint. Softly it spread, the brown stain astonishingly like the original. From his point of view, it seemed that the Shroud was to be no more than a huge water-colour.

Having found a way of creating the right colour, he now needed the right base for it. Could he find a linen cloth of the correct herringbone pattern? He contacted the Irish Linen Advisory Centre – and very soon his optimistic convictions about contemporary technology had received something of a dent. There were, he was told, several linens of the right date the quality of which was such that they could no longer be produced. In the matter of textiles, it seemed, mankind had taken something of a backward step since the first century AD.

The only herringbone weave of the right weight John Weston could find was unsuitable because it was green. It was apparently very popular with the Italian makers of lightweight suits but was useless for his purpose. He searched everywhere – through the stocks of his wife's shop, through those of a friend who ran a stall in Kingston market, through the shelves of every West End store. The experts of the Linen Advisory Centre, who had been very helpful, said they could arrange for a special bolt of the cloth to be woven, but it would take a long time and be very expensive. John knew that there was neither the time or the money to spare.

In the end, abandoning the absolute fidelity that

demanded a herringbone weave, he began to search simply for a cloth of the right general description. To his surprise, the one that most closely resembled the ideal turned out to be a man-made fibre with the trade name Trevira. This was soft, pliable, light and very near to linen. Its only drawback, from his point of view, was that it was white, a bright, lucent white very different from the time-darkened ivory of the Shroud.

Now his wife took a hand. She knew about textiles and their colouring. She began to experiment with various materials – coffee, for example, iodine, various commercial dyes. It was these last that she finally relied on, but in a shade she herself mixed, working with a painter's precision as she strove to create the delicate blend John needed. When she was satisfied, she put her mixture in a washing machine, then thrust the fourteen feet of the replica Shroud into it.

The next problem neither she nor John had foreseen. How do you dry a recently dyed fourteen-foot long strip of material without making creases in which the colour can collect? They hung the Trevira out of a bedroom window, in order to keep it clear of the ground. At frequent intervals, they would shake it, making it flap as though in a breeze; they had to keep it agitated if the dye was to remain even. It was fortunate that this was summer and that, in a year of mixed weather, they were in the middle of a warm spell. The cloth dried relatively swiftly; the time had come to try and replicate the image.

The size of the Shroud was again the first difficulty to be overcome. In his house near Ham, John began to rearrange his family's accommodation. He moved his children out of their bedroom, overriding all protests with appeals to the common interest. He put their beds in his own office and workroom; the space thus freed he filled with an enormous trestle table. Its working surface was a piece of chipboard eight feet long, so that by pinning down the cloth he was able to work on one half of the complete image, first the front view, then the back.

His opening move was to lay tracing paper over the cloth. On this he placed a full-sized photograph of the Shroud. Very carefully, he traced the image in all its details, and the details of the ancient cloth's every mark and scar. Then he dampened a tiny section of the material, and to this patch applied his small, meticulous brush. Often, once the colour had completed its slow spread, he would have to wait for it to dry before he could continue. On the wet base, the red-brown lines and stains looked heavier, clumsier, above all darker than they did once the material had dried. He had no idea how much colour he had actually put on, nor how deeply or faintly it had stained the material. Occasionally, of course, he made a mistake, and then he was grateful for the hardihood of the textile he had chosen. Several times he had to scrub it right down to its pale, ochre base again, but it never showed any sign of wear. Once, searching for a way to cut the time he was spending, he bleached out an error. Unfortunately, the colour bleached out as well, leaving a single bright patch that seemed to shame the ivory dullness of the rest. It had to be swiftly redyed.

The work stretched through the hot, airless days. He worked, stripped to the waist, dabbing and dabbing at the cloth with his small brush, covering it a square inch or two at a time. Only by keeping to such small areas could he be sure of reproducing the necessary detail. David's reaction when he saw the finished front view did much to encourage him. 'Great! Marvellous, exactly what we wanted. Exactly!'

Five weeks of unremitting work brought the replica to a finish. John showed it to David again, then took it down to Bristol and displayed it for Ian Wilson. It was Wilson who had given him the essential clue to the colour of the image. 'Remember the scorch marks on an ironing cloth and aim for something like that'. He had also sent him photographs with colour references that corrected errors of printing. Now, with the expert eye of one who had seen the original, he examined John's version of the Shroud and gave it his approval. Back in London, David praised the replica again, then said, 'And now we need another'. John stared at him, aghast. But David was firm – they needed to have in the film shots of the Shroud as it had been before fire had marked it. Thus for another twenty days or so John returned to his labours. At the end of that period *The Silent Witness* had its necessary armoury of replicas. John Weston's ingenuity had proven itself in yet another test.

There were no more preparations to make. The director, the production manager and the crew were gathered, primed, ready to depart. In Turkey, Samim awaited them. In France, Patricia Warren, whom David had met during a Cannes Film Festival and who lived in the country, was making the final arrangements for their arrival. The dollar-based funding had been established. In the United States, the interested participants awaited with patience the consequences of what they had supported. In Colorado, in Los Angeles, in Rome and Zurich, in Cambridge and Bristol, the film's active participants stood by for their calls. For David, the moment had come to take a deep breath and make his final plunge towards the finishing tape.

THE FILMING

The politics were over. If there had been evasions, diplomatic reconstruction of the facts or a glossing over of inconvenient opinions, now the time had come to tell the truth. The shifts David had occasionally been brought to in order to get the cameras turning were no longer of importance. It was not on these that his integrity would be judged but on what the screen displayed. He may have talked and wheedled and argued his way towards this moment, but the time of compromise was over. He and his overwhelming subject were at last directly to confront each other.

In many ways, of course, this simplified his task. He was in charge now. Naturally he had to consider his team, and the individuals who were to appear in the film, but he was the one whose decisions would count. Filming was to begin in France: they would shoot the early scenes in Chambéry and Lirey, the locations where the Shroud had first been seen in Europe. Then they would move on to Turkey, for the Byzantine scenes in Istanbul and the Edessa scenes in Urfa. On the way back they would halt in Rome to film Monsignor Ricci. Turin would await another journey, as would the English scenes and those in the United States. Later, there would be filming in a studio, recreating such sequences as were needed – the studio of Secondo Pia, say, or scenes from the Passion of Christ. They would need actors for these, an art director capable of designing the necessary sets and craftsmen who could build them.

The immediate task, however, was to arrange and execute the first stage of this operation. The papers make their own witness of how meticulous the preparatory work was. The itineraries lie neatly on the page, impressive in their certainty: 'David Rolfe/Roger Connolly/Bahram Manocheri/L. Prinz/Marion Allison and all photographic equipment leave London for Paris, France ... The above personnel will then transfer to Le Bourget Airport ... Patricia Warren, our French Location Coordinator, will meet crew at hotel ... Filming in Chambéry ... Entire unit ... with all photographic equipment leave France for Turkey, via Switzerland ... Samin Deger, our Turkish Location Coordinator, will meet the crew at Istanbul Airport ... Entire crew will film in Istanbul ... Entire crew, including Samin Deger, Dr Max Frei and local technicians ... will depart Istanbul Airport to Gazientep via Ankara ... At Gazientep Airport, road transportation ... will drive entire crew and their equipment to Urfa ...' Thus the schedule, flimsy barrier against the boisterous gales of real life.

Friday, 29 July, 1977, was the date fixed for the crew's departure to Paris: 'Flight BE 016, dep. Heathrow 14.00', read the itinerary. On the Tuesday before, a telex arrived at David's London office. The permissions to film in Turkey, so carefully gathered by Salim Deger, had been abruptly rescinded. They would not be allowed to shoot in Istanbul, nor would they be allowed near Urfa, which lay within a military zone. David stared at the message. It made no sense. He was committed: he had spent thousands of pounds, had engaged the crew, hired the equipment and booked the flights – he could neither cancel nor reorganise. Frantically, he cabled Samin Deger and then contacted the Foreign Office.

They were explanatory without being particularly helpful. The Centre-Left government of Bulen Ecevit had fallen. With it had vanished its freer, more liberal attitudes (a relative term – it was Ecevit who had ordered the Cyprus invasion). A Right-wing coalition under Demirel had taken power, and, in an Islamic country, the Right included strong elements of Muslim orthodoxy. It was almost certainly these, suspicious of a Western film crew engaged in a manifestly Christian endeavour, which had blocked David's plans and withdrawn the permits. It looked as if he had become the latest victim of the Crusades.

He felt as though he were suddenly surrounded by wreckage. The proposed itinerary was based on the most practical considerations – a journey that began in France, continued to Urfa, the farthest point East, and then returned by way of Rome could be accommodated on a single round ticket. To reverse the Turkish and Italian legs of the trip would be to add vastly to the expense, even if such a late alteration was possible. To cancel the whole of the planned shooting until the problem with the Turkish government had been solved would be even more costly. He was paying valuable technicians daily money of a kind that would soon reduce his resources to ludicrous proportions. If he dismissed them, on the other hand, he would be faced in a few weeks or, at worst, a few months, with the task of gathering a completely new crew. And what would his standing be with Harry John or with Monsignor Ricci, waiting to be filmed in Rome, if at this first practical demonstration of his abilities the result were to be failure, stalemate, silence, immobility?

Meanwhile, the British Embassy in Istanbul, which he had contacted, had sent him a telex, urbanely agreeing to intervene without offering much hope that such an intervention would really help. Deger was being more reassuring. He was certain he would be able to find a way round the problem; David was not to be too concerned. There were always solutions, new routes when old pathways closed. This oriental optimism seemed somewhat dubious to David, but his choices were limited. Although his Turkish agent clearly had something to gain by reassuring him and so staying in employment, he had impressed David with his energy and resourcefulness. Taking a deep breath, he decided to trust Salim's optimism. The plans would stand. They would leave on the 29th. To do nothing would be to admit failure. If he was to do something, however, then this was the only something he could do.

When the crew flew off to Paris, however, David was handicapped not only by uncertainty about what was happening in Turkey, but also by an injured foot. Batting in a cricket match, he had swung at the ball and missed; off-balance, he had stamped on his own foot and ankle so heavily that the injuries caused by his boot-studs were not to heal for another two months. He was to spend the weeks of filming hobbling on a stick ... A late arrival then, in their Chambéry hotel (alleviated, though, by the crew's finding in their rooms small gifts of sweets and flowers, arranged by their local co-ordinator, Patricia Warren) and, the next morning, deep gloom descending to match the weather outside. For David, staring moodily at the rain, Istanbul on his mind and his foot in bandages, this turn in the weather seemed like one more humourless trick played by a malicious providence.

If he believed it to be the last, he was soon to be disabused. The director he had chosen was beginning to behave as though already the strain of filming on location was more than he could bear. His conduct veered between the indecisive and the overbearing. He began to harass the cameraman, as though preparing to institute a tour-long vendetta. He had wanted his own with him, legitimately thwarted in this – equally legitimate – desire, he was taking resentment out on Bahram. Already on this first full day the tensions and arguments were burrowing into the harmony that was essential if they were to become an effective unit. If this were so at this early stage, in the relatively easy working conditions of central France, what would happen when they began to work in the heat, the red-brown dust and the general discomfort of Urfa?

A day spent checking and testing the equipment – and then, on a misty summer's morning, the camera at last began to turn. Through its impassive lens were sucked the roofs and façades of the city where, four centuries before, the Shroud had first been taken into the keeping of the House of Savoy. Here stood the Sainte Chapelle that had been built especially to house the relic. Here, among the western ramparts of the Alps, in this little town secure in its beautiful river valley, fire had struck at the Shroud. From here it had been carried along the banks of the River Arc and up, across the high pass, to Italy and Turin. All day they laboured to record on film the very walls and windows that had looked down on those distant caretakers of the Holy Shroud.

From Chambéry, the unit drove in three hired stationwagons to the ancient town of Troyes, their route winding down to the slow, grey Rhône and on through the wine-country of Burgundy, where in disciplined ranks the vintage of 1977 slowly ripened towards harvest. Troyes, once the capital of the Dukes of Champagne, was still the administrative centre of the department of Aube (and, incidentally, the place name from which derives that troy-weight long used for precious metals). It would be their headquarters for the filming of that significant hamlet, Lirey.

That evening they drove to the village on a reconnaissance. Roof ridges curved under the burden of centuries. A quiet so profound it was as though, if one listened carefully, one might still hear the excited trumpets sounding, all those centuries ago for the first time when the Holy Shroud had been held up before the dazzled eyes of Frenchmen. A tumbledown church; but no vestige of the original wooden abbey Geoffrey de Charny had built to house his miraculous cloth. Heavy trees all about, and birdsong. No traffic, no commerce – not even a village shop. Only the *maire*, busily at their command, anxious to display friendship, and energetically inviting them to a civic luncheon next day. As they drove back to Troyes, where five hundred years earlier Pierre d'Arcis had scribbled down his outrage at what he considered fraud, one might have thought from their smiles that everything was going well for them.

Perhaps the filming was; at least it had begun. But within the unit, the discontents of the director were causing increasing problems. Bahram, a gentle person, was finally provoked into retaliatory anger. Thus, at midnight the sleepy corridors of their family hotel were momentarily enlived by the cannonading temperaments of a film crew on the road. David, witnessing the disturbance, had no doubt at all that it was with the director that the fault lay.

Even if the case had not seemed so clear cut, a director has the responsibility of his position – and that includes the task of keeping the crew actively participant, happy to work to his instructions and their morale as high as their involvement is intense. At the very least, he has to ensure that he does not by his manner induce a general mulishness – that can soon degenerate into a greater or lesser refusal to cooperate. If such a point is reached, the venture is in jeopardy. A small film crew on location achieves success only by everybody doing a little more than the merely necessary. Ideally, it becomes a group of people united in a single purpose – and it is the director above all who must unite them. It is he who works in the closest intimacy with them; the producer, although a part of the team, has powers over money supply and employment that inevitably set him apart from the others. A director who nags, who is indecisive, who selects victims on whom to vent his unprovoked resentment, is in danger of sabotaging the entire progress of the film. David seemed to have picked such a director, or so he felt. And there remained Turkey, looming ahead of them like a rocky coast before a vessel under sail.

David decided to speak with Connolly, the production manager, who must have reached some conclusions about the state of morale in the unit and would know what the crew really thought. If he were nervous about broaching so explosive a subject, Connolly was unreservedly relieved that he had done so. Everybody, he told David, was very unhappy with the situation. It made them uneasy and – whether out of a sense of justice or because Bahram was their colleague – they blamed the director for having created it. Alone in his own room, David pondered the matter. Either the director or Bahram would have to go, they could not continue as they had begun. Only two days into their schedule the whole enterprise was already beginning to fall apart. The relationship of a producer to a director when circumstances like these arise is simple: he has only two alternatives and the phrase that sums them up is 'Sack or back'. Could he back a director whom everyone thought at fault? Why should he? Just because he *was* the director? If he did back him, Bahram would have to go. Where would one find another camera-lighting man to replace him – and how long would such replacement take? On the other hand, if David let the director go, who would orchestrate the work? But even as he posed the question, he knew the answer. For a moment, pacing to and fro, he stared into the mirror. His reflection peered expressionlessly back.

"That's who", he said. He picked up the telephone and dialled the director's room. A small wind moved heavy branches in the darkness; a shutter creaked gently; a car, then a motor-cycle, passed in the distance. The night pressed heavily upon these tiny sounds, burying them in a deep silence that seemed to belong to an earlier time when people were sparser on the earth ... The director, his disgruntled voice hoarse with fatigue, spoke into his ear. David said, "I'm afraid I've some bad news for you. I'm going to let you go ... Yes. Fired. Yes, I'm afraid so ... Oh, yes – I have the right ... No, there's no point in discussing it ..."

Too restless even to lie on his bed, David went out, hobbling on his stick through the narrow streets and shuttered shopping precincts of the city. Would he be able to undertake what had now been so abruptly thrust on him? He had hired a director precisely because, after more than two years with the project, he doubted the freshness of his eye, of his ideas. Now, however, as he wandered down the curving, empty pavements, he found that his imagination was quickening to the challenge. He began in his mind to put together sequences, to consider alternatives, angles, approaches – he began once again to *see* his film, as he had done at the very beginning. A little calmer, easier in his mind, he returned to the hotel; quite soon, he drifted off into the sleep he craved. It was half past three in the morning.

At five o'clock, there came the awakening knock on his door. They had to make an early start if they were to finish their work in Lirey that day. When he opened the door, David was astonished to find the director there, script in hand just as though last night's conversation had not taken place at all. If he had believed that David's decision had been made in haste, a matter of darkness and depression which the morning would cure, he soon found he was mistaken. And he had made another error by bringing Bahram himself to plead for him. Bahram's generosity did him credit and might in some circumstances have had an effect. But David realised that if he knew about the dismissal, so did the rest of the unit. Two conclusions followed from this: first, knowing the director had already been dismissed once, the crew were bound to have their remaining respect for him undermined; second, knowing that their producer had been persuaded to reinstate him, his credibility, too, would be seriously weakened. The result was certain to be a possibly catastrophic loss of efficiency.

At this point it has to be remembered that David was only twenty-six, in charge of his first real film of any size. He was the youngest person in the unit. The assertion and maintenance of his authority must sometimes have seemed to him more difficult and therefore more important than it would have been for someone older and more established. He could not afford to appear indecisive, even if he had wanted to change his mind. As it happened, he did not. Firmly, he stood by the decision he had made. Later, in Lirey itself, the director was to make one more attempt to be reinstated; faced with David's adamantine certainty, however, he had no alternative but to return (Insouciant? Sullen? Furious?) to England. David had come through the first great crisis of the filming. How would he manage with those still to arise, now that he had taken on dual responsibilities? No one wondered more fervently than he.

In Lirey, sunshine brought a rich glow to ancient roof-tiles. As the camera was being set up, David became aware of his eagerness to get to work. For months, he had been forced to consider *The Silent Witness* as a business venture, as a fundamentally verbal investigation, as an exercise in logistics. Now, his eye refreshed by having been thus distracted, he could treat it purely as a film again. He was sustained, too, by the support of the crew, who – he now realised – had for forty-eight hours considered the director's eventual dismissal as probable, even inevitable. In the thin diffused light of early morning, he and they went to work with a will.

A sense of time. A sense of the lushness of the land. A sense of mystery, of a strange moment when, without precedent or warning, this place had become the scene of that first, awe-inspiring exposition. Dawn brightened the fields heavy with ripening wheat. The camera scanned their riches, trapped and caught them, as the corn glistened through the summer-heavy trees: the church, haunting in its decay, glimpsed through an opening door, a window; the tower marching towards heaven, the contented houses, pressed down by the weight of centuries. Thus, on his first day's shooting, David and his camera crew sucked in and imprisoned the images they desired. And then it was time for lunch.

Everyone came, it seemed. As the unit drove to the mayor's house, they were accompanied by the three beaming *gendarmes* the authorities had supplied. All morning, these burdened policemen had cleared the roads – the roads of Lirey where two girls skipping made a crowd! – and controlled the traffic – the traffic of Lirey, where three cars in an hour meant congestion! – and now they were going to make sure that these strangers would find their way without mishap through the complexities of the hamlet's streets. Safely, therefore, they came to a large, modern house on the outskirts and, even without help, would probably have been able to find their way through the cool interior into the brilliant garden beyond.

Lawns, shrubs, flowers, with sunshine over all – trestle tables in the shade, green and brilliance reflected in glass, in cutlery – the bottles ready on the table, those and the others placed ready, beaded with moisture: champagne bottles, what else? – and the wide glasses already filled, already refilled. Then the twelve courses, the patés and the salads and the *gigot* and the cheese and the fruits, fetched and eaten and carried away as the voices rose and the laughter silenced the birds. Then, naturally, the speeches: *M. le maire* was honoured, he was delighted, he was filled with pride that his little village ... And then David, for his part, was more than grateful; he was overwhelmed by the friendliness and the hospitality and was filled, it went without saying, with admiration for the beauty, the calm, the history ... Bilingual applause, then, enough to send garden pests cowering under the leaves, for everyone could see that the speeches were over and one or two, perhaps, had even heard them; but there were still bottles to empty, that was the important thing, and nobody was going to leave until that matter had been attended to.

Only Roger Connolly, conscientious among the debris, shooting schedules on his mind, was in honourable despair. How were they to do the filming that was still planned? Cigar smoke lifted on the heavy air, its scent vying with the roses. Heroically, he continued to urge a return to work. And, indeed, at five o'clock they did at last unsteadily set themselves to use the last hours of daylight, but willingness of spirit was defeated by the obduracy of the flesh. Zooms started too late, progressed too unsteadily and stopped too soon; focus lost its sharpness; pans sagged away into blurred close-ups of the ground; professionalism dwindled into lack of expertise; they would have been baffled by a seaside snapshot. There was nothing for it but to pack up and hope that what they had would be sufficient – as, of course, it was. With the farewells of Lirey resounding in their memories, they drove giggling back to Troyes.

Thirty thousand feet below the port-side windows, the plains and ridges of the Balkans spread away to the north until they vanished in a blue-grey haze. The evening held back, waited. Turkey lay ahead – and what traumas, David wondered, lay ready hatched in Turkey? In Paris he had received the copy of a telex from the British embassy in Ankara. It confirmed the doubtfulness of the situation and added that a film crew recently discovered working without a permit in Urfa had ended up in prison, with their equipment confiscated. He had passed that refreshing item on to the rest of the unit, then asked them what they felt about the risks. Should they go on or turn back? Unanimously, they had chosen to continue – a consequence, he felt, of a new solidarity, a new commitment, brought about by the dramas they had passed through in Troyes and Lirey. The director's dismissal, followed by that epic meal in the mayor's garden, had cemented them into a team. They had been through problems together now; they had a history: one could turn round to a companion and say, 'Hey, do you remember ...?'

All the same, as the airliner sped on above an Aegean Sea already darkening for the night, David could not turn aside the questions nagging him; nor did the moist, oppressive heat of Istanbul Airport at first offer any relief. Then, looking around, he suddenly saw a familiar smile – Samim among the crowd, giving him the thumbs-up sign of optimism. With the Customs officials they went through the lengthy and sometimes acrimonious negotiations that seem inseparable from the transportation of film equipment across frontiers, until finally they were free to travel into the city (though temporarily without their boxed, complicated gear). And David, relaxing in his hotel room, at last discovered the reason for Samim's unexpected satisfaction.

It turned out to be remarkably sound. Samim had presented himself at the Ministry of Culture as a wealthy producer anxious to make a film about his native land:

indeed, its title was to be *My Country*. He had told the officials that in order to ensure that its quality would do justice to its subject, the Turkish crew would be reinforced by British technicians. These had already been hired and were soon to arrive. He produced for the Ministry his list of desired locations – including the very ones, of course, that David had earlier specified. The bureaucrats were delighted: their function, after all, was to promote the historical arts and beauties of Turkey. Without the least debate, they issued the necessary permits. The crew of *My Country* was free to film the monuments and mosques it desired.

The only snag was that David would not be able, at least overtly, to direct. Nor could his British crew be too much in evidence among the extra Turkish technicians Samim had had to hire – though Bahram, as an Iranian, was not likely to be noticeable among them. It was David himself who would have to keep his distance – Samim had to be 'director' or suspicions would be aroused. Police might be assigned to them, though in the most useful capacity possible – to keep crowds away, smooth communications, ensure security – but official friendliness would be dangerously modified by any sign of trickery. To this slightly deflating scheme David was glad to agree; it might involve a curiously long-distance way of directing his film, but it would at least get him the shots he needed without waiting for the Turkish bureaucrats to come to a decision. At a little conference held the next morning in the bare room set aside for their equipment, the whole unit agreed to co-operate in the subterfuge.

Shooting began the following day. As Sue Summers, who reported on their operation, wrote in *Screen International*, 'Coincidentally, *My Country*, as the clapperboard had it, took in the same locations as *The Silent Witness*. Though British people hung about with 35mm cameras, light meters and Uhers, they were, you understand, just tourists. This guise worked perfectly in Istanbul – even when shooting just a few yards from a military observation post.' There were other hazards, however. The film called for interior shots of Saint Sophia, the vast cathedral built by the Emperor Justinian in the sixth century. Its architectural wonder of a dome and the four minarets set up by the Ottoman conquerors who turned it into a mosque, have dominated the Istanbul skyline for centuries. The artists of Byzantium had decorated it with glass-mosaic panels, and even today, with this miraculous building a museum, some of them still shimmer on the ancient walls. David needed to include these in his Constantinople sequence. To counter the proper ecclesiastical gloom that surrounded them, however, he would have to instal lights, the special lamps that offer sunray intensities to film makers.

Lamps of that sort take time to set up. The lighting of a huge space – the inside of a cathedral, say – is a matter for great expertise exercised through a long process of trial and error. The custodian of St Sophia's gave them exactly one hour. Neither Ministry of Culture permits nor such bribes as they could afford would sway him in the least. They could begin at a quarter past five; at a quarter past six, they would have to pack up. Samim engaged every spare electrician and hired every spare light that he could find. The men worked as though employed by Justinian himself. Cables coiled viperously across the flagstoned floor. From unexpected shelves and crannies there gleamed the glass-and-aluminium lustre of the lamps. Shirt-sleeved experts clambered into impossible positions, twisted wire into unlikely connections, guessed in a minute falls of radiance that in a studio they would have studied for an hour. At ten minutes past six, David took a deep and perhaps querulous breath. 'Lights!' he yelled.

The ancient generators began to throb. The lamps blazed out. Bahram, excited to be among the few who had filmed the St Sophia interior, tilted his camera and began to focus on the mosaics. They glittered with a brilliance that can surely have been matched only rarely in the fifteen centuries of their existence. Alas, it was a brief, butterfly irridescence: abruptly, everything went dark Had there been an explosion? Dazzled eyes stared blankly around. Someone came running in from outside – all visible lights, in house or street, had in that instant gone out. Indeed, as they heard later, all the lights in the district had blinked off at the same moment. But was it they who had overloaded the system? Or was it only a powercut, normal enough in Istanbul, that had incidentally doused their lamps, too? They might have found out, with effort, but thought it hardly worth bothering the authorities. Busy people, authorities – and who knew what they might want to know in return?

So they filmed by normal light after all – Bahram had remembered a special process used in the United States; the film would have to be sent to an American laboratory, but that was a small price to pay for getting the necessary shots. Then, without too much fuss, they packed up to return to their hotel. They had almost finished in Istanbul and would soon be on their way to do the three days' scheduled filming that awaited them in Urfa. Awaited them, that is, if they could circumvent the civil authorities, the police, the military ... Meanwhile, David hurried back to meet Max Frei. He would travel on with them, so that near Urfa they might reconstruct and film the researches he had actually done in Israel.

They had arranged to meet in the hotel dining-room. David ate while he was waiting, sharing with Connolly a table in sight of the door. Beyond the heavy plate-glass windows the lights of Taksim Square shone faintly through the filmy curtains. He felt both pleased and anxious. Their work had gone well in Istanbul, but what hazards awaited them in Urfa? Connolly nodded at the door. Dr Frei had come in. The Swiss smiled as he saw them and waved a greeting. He walked towards them, his hand outstretched. David, leaning on his stick, bent forward to shake it. Beside him, sudden hammers smashed into the glass.

The windows began to fall inward, thundering: crystal

rain arched, then scattered. A man nearby began an urgent, insistent bellowing, a dark counterpoint to the screams of women. Outside, the vast hammering continued. Without stopping, David, still reaching forward, continued his movement until he lay spreadeagled on the floor.

'It's shooting!' he cried. 'Someone's shooting at us!'

Across the room, the glasses on a waiter's tray suddenly leaped and crumbled. Distracted, a woman ran, screaming, her fingers clawing at her hair. Everywhere diners were flinging themselves to the scant safety of the floor. Someone pulled down the running woman. Out of sight, her voice continued its high, hysterical keening. A man, prone under the next table, was grumbling in a low, nervous monotone, 'Been all round the world. All round the world, you know. But I've never been in anything like this. Never.' Two men – later David learned they were veterans of the Vietnam war – were expertly snaking their way across the carpet towards the door and safety.

Abruptly, people began to realise that there had been silence for some time. They rose to their knees, then to their feet and looked about them. In low voices at first, then with the volume of urgency, they asked again and again, 'What happened? Who was it? Who shot at us?' All around lay the debris of this event that had so altered their evening. Not for long, however. With an aplomb one might have thought the result of long practice, the clearing up began. Glass was swept away, and broken china; tables were straightened, chairs rearranged, guests soothed. Within half an hour only the missing window panes indicated the drama that had interrupted the expensive hotel calm.

Earlier that year, on May Day, students had staged a massive rally in Istanbul. Thousands of them had gathered in Taksim Square to protest against the ugly repressions of the régime. The government had countered, as such governments do, with a ferocity that both justified and exceeded the violence of the demonstrators. They had ordered the military to shoot into the crowd; thirty-four people had died. In that operation, the hotel had been a command post. It was for that reason, therefore, that on the evening of David's rendezvous with Dr Frei a motorcycle had roared across the square and then pulled in to the kerb. The rider on the pillion had lifted a sub-machine-gun. While the engine roared, he had put burst after burst into the flamboyant bourgeois comforts of the restaurant. Then, before anyone had even thought of retaliation or alarms, the motorcycle had swung away into the dusk, vanishing in the endless lanes and alleys of the city. The whole incident had taken less than a minute; by the time the film crew came back from their own adventures, it already seemed incredible. It was only the bullet scars on the metal boxes in their first-floor equipment room that finally convinced them that David was telling the truth.

As for him, he was beginning to feel that, whatever crisis lurked in wait for them in Urfa, after what had already happened it could only turn out to be an anti-climax.

It was Samim who bore the brunt of diplomatic activity now. The film they had come to make was, after all, ostensibly his. David had the duty of behaving as much like a tourist as possible. The staff of his hotel, his family and familiarly awful Kapakli Hotel, may have known that he was there to supervise the camera-work, but they were friends of his by now and not prepared to discuss him with the authorities. The nights were hot and stuffy, sleep kept at bay not only by the absence of air-conditioning but by the presence below his window of the local 'labour exchange' where workers waited to be chosen by potential employers. They would arrive early in the morning, often before dawn; those disappointed would remain long into the night, dramatically discussing the melancholy facts of their situation.

Nevertheless, every morning David would stroll through the streets with Samim, discussing with him the sequences to be tackled that day. Although Samim had spoken with the local *khalif* and obtained the necessary permits, everyone remained understandably nervous – Turkish security forces had a tendency to open enquiries by shooting the suspect. David had forsaken the use of their long zoom lens with its threatening barrel because of a fear that the military might take it for some sort of bazooka and cut them down with 'retaliatory' fire. Four policemen had been assigned to the unit supposedly shooting Samim's *My Country*, two in uniform and two in plain clothes, and under this protective surveillance it was essential that David and the rest of the British members of the crew kept their parts in the filming to a minimum and always of an apparently subordinate nature.

The person most involved in this deception, apart from Samim, was the cameraman, Bahram. David had insisted that he control the shots, since his skills were essential to ensure the quality of the finished film. It was decided to pass him off as a Turk, a device that was implausible in only one respect: Bahram spoke no Turkish. It had been necessary to create for him a new personality, as it were – that of the dedicated, single-minded artist, preoccupied with his craft and surly to the point of silent indifference when approached. If one of the policemen or a curious bystander tried to speak with him, Samim or another of the crew would dart forward to intervene. 'Please, he hates chattering while he's working ... he has eyes for his shot and nothing else ... please don't ask him any questions; he's liable to walk off, go on strike ... Now what was it you wanted to know?' Impressed at such a romantic involvement with the task in hand, the interrupter would allow himself to be diverted. But even after the first day the strain was beginning to tell on Bahram, who, in fact, is sensitive, highly strung and dedicated. It was as well that their schedule called for a stay of only three days.

David, frustrated at having to leave the minute-by-minute supervision of the shooting to Samim but, in the circumstances, delighted that any shooting at all was going on, found that time, in a small city now so familiar, tended to drag. He changed his room for one with a balcony. His nights were now noisier but cooler. There was also an unexpected advantage – across the road there was an open-air cinema. From his balcony he could watch the flickering of distant film stars as they went about their dazzling love-affairs and melodramas. All about him in the dark, the reflected blue-white light glowed eeerily from the eyes and grinning teeth of Urfa's agile citizenry. They clung to every ledge and cranny as, with him, they took their free share of these delights.

David's own filming went ahead unexpectedly swiftly and efficiently. In one morning the unit filmed the weaving of the Shroud. The gnarled old master-weaver spent almost the whole time lamenting the smallness of his fee. He had been paid £350 for the use of his workroom for half a day; all his friends, however, had been assuring him for weeks that this was a tiny sum to receive from a film company and that he had been cheated. According to Samim, this is a local custom – one must try to persuade anyone who has had a stroke of luck that his fortune is not as good as he had imagined. In the case of this sour weaver, with his seamed face and baggy trousers, the persuasion had worked and, with two years' income in his pocket, he wept that it was not more. His work would be disrupted, he wailed; his consignments late; above all, his women would be disgraced by the eyes of strangers and, what was worse, foreigners. 'I should have been given thousands!' he shouted, in a tantrum. 'I should have been given thousands. Thousands!' By salutary contrast, the man who actually did the work, and who appears in the film, almost wept with gratitude when David paid him £12 – equivalent to his wages for two months.

In the evenings, they ate in the cool of the open air, in rooftop restaurants hazy with the smoke from charcoal grills. There were fruits of every kind, and salads crisply fresh, fat olives and white cheese, tiny cups of black, near-solid coffee. Most of the people they met took them to be Germans, the long connection between Germany and

Turkey making that the most likely. Shouting 'Alman! Alman!' young boys would run after them in the streets, begging or offering, with uninhibited gestures, the simpler kinds of sexual gratification.

The filming of Max Frei posed problems. It had to be done outside the city, which might by itself have caused difficulties in a military zone. But there was the added factor of explaining what Dr Frei was doing at all in a film entitled *My Country*. The best way around that was to make sure that no one asked. First of all, however, they had to find a suitable location, the one they had earmarked during their reconnaissance having proved too lush and too distant to be used. One was found, not far from the citadel that dominated the town; roads ran near it, but by shooting between them, the area appeared to the camera to be a wilderness – the very Wilderness of Judaea that they were attempting to recreate. In the heat, the scramble up the citadel slope taxed everyone – although there were those less agile than Marion, the continuity girl, by then, unknown to David, over three months pregnant.

In the film, Dr Frei wanders through authentic semi-desert, picking and clutching various small plants. Over his image, his Swiss sing-song floats: 'This plant is Suaeda. In this particular variety it is known only in Palestine. I found pollen from it on the Shroud ... And this here is Paganum Hamala, a desert plant that is very frequent between Jericho and the Dead Sea. I found pollen from this plant, too, on the Shroud ...' The sequence has drama and conviction. Introduced by a long shot of Jerusalem, it leaves no doubt of its authenticity in the minds of audiences.

When they had finished filming in Urfa, they flew back to Istanbul. Turkey had still one more problem to set them – how were they to take out with them reels shot for British film named *The Silent Witness* when all of them had ostensibly been shooting material for a Turkish film entitled *My Country*? They had left their Istanbul sequences in Samim's mother's refrigerator – had they run into real trouble in Urfa, Samim might eventually have been able to smuggle them out. Now, with what they had shot in Anatolia, they packed them in a box. Their still unexposed stock they placed in another. Then they left for the airport and the flight that would – if they caught it – take them on to Rome and Monsignor Ricci.

They soon discovered that they had not given way to exaggerated fears. The officials flatly refused to believe the story they had decided on – that they had been trying to obtain permits, had failed in this despite days of endeavour, and consequently, in a mood of frustration and bitterness, were about to shake off the dust of Turkey for ever. The Customs impounded all their film. That, at least, was their intention – what they actually confiscated was the box of unused stock. The exposed reels, in their cardboard box (about a foot square and lined with X-ray protection), were actually on the ground between Marion's feet, hidden by her fashionably long skirt.

Was it the low position women have traditionally held in Turkish society that left her unwatched and unmolested? David now believes so. Inch by inch she made her way towards the doorways that led to the airliners and freedom. The box between her feet, sometimes surreptitiously thrust forward, as though by some maniacally secretive footballer, at others held between her feet like a penguin's egg, escaped all notice, nor did anyone consider peculiar her bizarre and almost imperceptible progress across the hall. At last, and in the course of a long, tense time, her feet made the final thrust. Goal! She had scored the decider for her team.

Everything else, however, was still in the Customs officers' hands. Somewhere outside, David knew, Marion and the precious box, now guarded by the rest of the unit, would be settling into their seats on their Pan Am flight to Rome. David had decided that they should travel on, while he and Connolly stayed with Samim and tried to free the equipment. He himself transferred to a Turkish

Airlines flight, however, when a seat became available, feeling that, like the general of a threatened army, he was the one indispensable person. If the affair ended in arrests, everyone but he was, in the last analysis, replaceable. Engine failure, however, forced him back to the continuing crisis and to a Roger Connolly who has, he feels, not even yet totally forgiven him for being left in so exposed a situation.

It was Samim who, as so often before, managed to arrange an unofficial solution. The officer in charge of their equipment was persuaded to experience a convenently sudden urge to seek the toilets. The next airliner for Rome was due to leave in ten minutes. The three men tugged and heaved and pulled, sweating as they hurled the heavy boxes on the luggage conveyor. Swift thanks and breathless farewells for the endlessly resourceful, endlessly invaluable Samim, and then David and Roger were racing through the departure lounge. They glimpsed through a window their luggage being loaded and sprinted for the cabin door. Finally airborne, their relief was that of men who had survived disaster. They had had to leave their film-stock behind, several thousand pounds' worth, but what they had shot was safe, and so was their equipment – and so were they. As the plane levelled out and headed briskly westward, they toasted their success with an understandable cheerfulness.

Three months later, with almost the whole film shot and Instanbul little more than an occasional disturbing memory, David finally received his permit to film in Turkey.

In Rome, there was only the interview with Monsignor Ricci to shoot. Predictably this was less simple than it might have seemed, partly because Monsignor Ricci, having spent a lifetime developing his elaborate theories, saw no reason to confine his exposition of them to the one minute David at first assigned him. What David wanted was for Monsignor Ricci to analyse the marks of flagellation borne by the man in the Shroud, once these had been objectively described in the pathologist's testimony. What Monsignor Ricci wanted, on the other hand, was a platform for further disseminating his own ideas. Once he was launched it was not easy to persuade him to halt; he spoke in his lecture room, in his study, on his shrubberied terrace. Resignedly, David let him have his head – his own time would come when the editor picked up his scissors.

In the film, Monsignor Ricci is tethered, firmly and very convincingly, to the evidence as defined by Dr Bucklin. In his analysis and extension of this, what he has to say is fascinating. He holds a whip, fitting its lashes to the wound shown in the image. The lashes are weighted with vicious, sometimes especially sharpened, pieces of metal or bone. Monsignor Ricci tells us that the Romans called these *taccilli*. We see how precisely they fit the wounds. He says, 'If we apply this to the photos of the Shroud, you have a graphic documentation of the marks left by one of the strokes of the whip, and one only ... Complete examination of the Holy Shroud gives us two scourges because the directions converge, one from the right and one from the left. And the number of strokes is excessive – more than a hundred and twenty.'

He shows us the marks on the shoulders left by the heavy beam of the cross. 'There are contusions and lacerations from the scourging wounds, which spread under the weight of the beam.' The man on the Shroud, like the man in the Bible, carried the means of his death to the place of his execution. On the way, he fell – the evidence is eloquent: 'His fall was unavoidable', Monsignor Ricci points out, now lecturing his students, 'and was one of the most common spectacles of those times. The consequences are very clear on the Shroud ... The left leg at the kneecap has a very bad laceration and contusion ...'

Finally, he deals with the headwounds, those tears and

scratches that seem to him of such significance. Sitting behind his desk, upright and very certain, his manner gravely convincing, he says, 'This wound, corresponding to the crown of thorns, probably more than any other identifies the man as Jesus Christ. The Gospels state clearly that the soldiers invented this torture for him alone ...'

David wanted to film Monsignor Ricci in the Vatican of which he has been so distinguished a servant. On St Peter's Square he set up a camera; in the shot, we see Monsignor Ricci at a distance, walking across that immense ecclesiastical plain. We are poised for a closer view, but it never comes. Before they could set up the second shot, the Vatican police had descended on them and neither their arguments nor the plaintive and later furious intervention of Monsignor Ricci could erode the determination of these custodians. The unit would have to leave. During the entire filming of this religious document, it is ironic that the only time they were forced to stop work it should have been by order of the Vatican police.

Now, home! Their first expedition was at an end. They had all worked without let-up, through the tensions of politics, climate and internecine disagreement. There were times in Rome when David felt that his crew was nearing mutiny. But that was over. 'I'll treat everyone to champagne', he cried in the Rome departure lounge. 'On the flight back – champers for everyone.' But their flight was delayed and a contrite British Airways eventually offered all their passengers free drinks, thus undermining his magnanimity. Still, champagne is champagne, never mind who's paying! As they drank, they played cards, signalling their bets by flashing their overhead lights. Thus, twinkling like a carnival, they descended into London.

For David there would be little remission of effort. He had so far seen not one foot of all the film that had been shot. What would its quality be? He was, after all, still a largely untried director. And what of the interview with

Monsignor Ricci? David had, after much thought, decided that he would have those taking part in the film speak directly to the camera. For people unused to this technique, it can be inhibiting, demanding, even harrowing. The neutrality of the camera's eye, the total indifference of its machine scrutiny, upsets those whose performance demands a human reaction. They miss the nods and smiles, the gasps of surprise or horror. Yet for an audience the results are much more accessible. There is not an unseen intermediary, somewhere in that unknown space to the left or right of the screen to whom these pregnant remarks are *really* being addressed. Instead of becoming eavesdroppers overhearing someone else's conversation, the spectators are spoken to directly. They are involved, a part of the total event.

On these grounds, David had arrived at his decision. Only now, however, was he to see whether it had brought him results. If it had not, he had a major problem – he could not go back and film Monsignor Ricci again; on the other hand, he could not easily change the style of the later interviews without changing this one, too. Breathlessly, therefore, he settled into the beguiling comfort of a viewing-theatre chair and waited for the first of his rushes to roll. Only when he had seen them all did he finally relax and allow himself a pale but satisfied smile. The work would do; it was usable; it was all right. They were still on course.

Now came the English filming. At Walsingham the Brotherhood of St Seraphim live in happy seclusion, painting icons according to the old traditions. It was there that David obtained the shots he needed for Ian Wilson's theory of the Mandylion-Shroud connection. 'To this day', the narrator tells us as the brush passes carefully across the wood, 'icon painters of the Eastern Church still base their work on copies of the Edessa Cloth, which they consider to be the true likeness.' An icon painted then still hangs, in sombre clarity, on the wall of David's office.

At Magdalene College, Oxford, it was arranged that

Ian Wilson should make his contribution. He was once more uncertain of David's intentions, having been made uneasy by the dismissal of the director. Nevertheless, a little tensely at first, then with greater ease and relaxation, he spoke about his ideas amid the polished wood and glowing leather of a room mellowed by hundreds of years of scholarship. 'I began to consider the simple fact that the likeness of Christ that has come down to us through the centuries was surprisingly similar to the image visible on the Shroud. I began to trace the likeness of Christ back through the centuries ... Right back, in fact to the sixth century, the likeness to the Shroud image was quite unmistakable. But before this there was a surprising inconsistency ... I wondered what was it that had brought about this sudden, definitive likeness in Christ's portraits from the sixth century on. Could it have been the Shroud?' And so his part of the investigation was set briskly in motion.

At Trinity College, Cambridge, in the airy study that was part workroom and part the sign of his authority, Dr Robinson, too, spoke his opinion to the camera. For him, a professional often under the demanding lights of a sound stage, this involved skills he had spent years developing. He spoke easily, with fluency, and followed with a hint of self-mockery the occasional instructions David gave him. His interest in the Shroud, he tells us, is that of a New Testament scholar. 'And I must confess that when I first investigated it I was as sceptical of this relic as of any other, all of which as far as I know have been shown to be bogus. But the more one went into it, the more one realised that there was so much about this thing that a forger would never really have thought of ... In fact what we have fits extraordinarily well with the New Testament evidence ... all I can say is that for me, the burden of proof has shifted. I began by assuming its inauthenticity until proved otherwise and asking how as a forgery it could possibly have been done. I now tend to assume that it's authentic – and still want to know how it was done.'

Filming in the village church of Templecombe followed, with its fresco of a bearded head, a relic of Templar days. Was this painting, so reminiscent of the Shroud image, a representation of that head upon which Templar worship and ritual was said to centre? The film descends into speculation here, as it must; but it is plausible speculation, at least. With this short sequence 'in the can', work on the British locations was for the moment finished.

It was August and time to leave on the next great leg of their adventure, their filming in the United States. The sound-man, Larry Prinz, a native of Los Angeles, flew ahead to use his local connections in hiring the equipment they needed – it seemed ridiculous to carry cameras from London to the world centre of film-making. David, meanwhile, once more made the somewhat drabber pilgrimage to mid-western Milwaukee, where Harry John and his de Rance Foundation awaited his report.

He arrived at the low building of the Foundation's headquarters at dusk. The doors were shut and locked; it was after eight o'clock in the evening. Looking upwards, David saw one lighted window. He yelled out, 'Harry! Harry!'

Shortly the window opened and the unpretentious millionaire pushed his head out. 'Oh – hello there, David. I'll get someone to open the door.' A few minutes later, David was settling into the now familiar office. They talked for two hours. Now that he was no longer making submissions and hoping for approval, David relaxed in the other man's presence. He could speak, not about what he hoped to achieve but about what he had done and was doing. He was no longer selling dreams but describing reality. Harry John seemed pleased with the film's progress – which was just as well, since he had a reputation for being litigious. He had fought members of his own family in the courts and had sued Rosselini, the famous Italian director, for making with a million dollars of de Rance money a film on Jesus which Harry John had found offensive – the revolutionary Jesus of Rosselini's vision was not likely to square with the ideas of an American, Mid-Western, Catholic industrialist. Thus, when they parted on the friendliest of terms, the silent building dark and faintly sinister about them, it is not surprising that David felt a certain sense of relief.

David had arranged to meet his wife and daughter, whom he had hardly seen for months, in Chicago, and from there they all flew on to Colorado Springs where the next stage of shooting was to take place. The United States Air Force Academy was in a festive bustle. They had arrived on one of the two great days of ceremony and parade which broke up the year. Flags flew everywhere, bands played, cadets as fresh as new-minted toys and as precise as robots marched in their ranged platoons across the grounds. Senior officers watched benignly from raised vantage points, rising at mysterious promptings to salute some parading section. Loudspeaker announcements harried or informed the crowds of mothers, fathers, lovers, spouses and assorted brothers and sisters who wandered in a daze of admiration around the edges of that vast, grass and asphalt stage.

David, his cinematographic fingers itching, could not wait to set up his camera. The only snag was that his sound-recording crew, assistant cameraman and continuity girl had all been held up in their journey by the air controllers' strike. He determined to shoot the scenes mute – they would have to find band music and crowd sounds to dub on later. As he was about to give the order to begin, he noticed running figures at the far edge of the enormous lawn, tiny yet but growing to the watching eye as they approached. His missing helpers, brought post-haste and in the nick of time by TWA. The scene was reminiscent of some last-reel rescue in a melodrama of the silent days.

Having set the general scene, David needed to show within it Captains Jackson and Jumper, the two scientists who were to appear in his film. To mark them out from those round about, he asked them to stand for a moment at the railing of the podium in their neat, pale blue shirts. It nearly brought disaster. 'Where are your jackets?' bawled some senior stickler, berating them with the easy fury of a man outraged by the trivial. By such military pedantry promotion is won – and through such military pedantry promotion can be lost. Threats thundered about the ears of the unfortunate scientists, leaving David with a burden of guilt – but later giving all three of them substantial cause for laughter.

The next day, they filmed the startling sequence, perhaps the heart of the film, in which Jackson and Jumper demonstrate some of their results. The camera had to be set up in a small laboratory jammed with electronic equipment, in which the two had conducted their experiments. No long shots were possible, nor very much of a general establishing shot, and every change of angle necessitated complex and irritating manoeuvring. It might have upset the scientists, but they co-operated with complete cheerfulness, saying their pieces into the camera with the ease of practised teachers.

They demonstrated the VP-8 Image Analyzer, centrepiece of their Albuquerque contribution, which, as Capt Jackson tells the audience, 'has the ability to translate the image patterns as adjustable levels of relief' – that is, can display on a monitor screen three-dimensional versions of certain two-dimensional images. Not all two-dimensional images, however. As Dr Jumper demonstrates, a fetching portrait in his hand: 'I have here an ordinary photograph of myself in mess dress, one which I'm sure my mother would be very proud of, and I'm going to put this under the camera.' On the monitor, a jumbled and distorted version of Capt Jumper instantly appears. 'I'm sure that you'll agree that even my mother would have trouble recognising me there. A normal photograph records only variations in light and does not record information about the distance the camera was from the subject.'

A photograph of the face of the man on the Shroud

produces a very different reaction. In an unearthly fluorescent green, the photograph of the Shroud image opens out into a bold three-dimensional version. Whoever the man was, his face, filled out into the dimensions of life, floats there on the screen, to be seen for the first time since ... But dates presume certainties, and one must not leap ahead of the evidence. Capt Jackson is pointing out to us, cautiously, 'This can only be explained if the intensity levels of the Shroud image itself are incoded with distance information from the cloth to the body.' The density of the picture on the Shroud, it seems (and as the audiences at Albuquerque had already learned), varies according to how far away from the cloth different parts of the body were – the nearer, the denser. What caused such an effect? Once more, speculation takes over. What cannot be disputed is the consequence – this phosphorescent image before us, turning in response to Captain Jackson's finger on the dials.

'When I first saw this image', he tells us, 'I think I knew how Seconda Pia must have felt when, in 1898, he saw his photographic image. As scientists, we believe that it would be practically impossible for a forger, much less a mediaeval one, to have produced an image like this.' Silently we watch as, very slowly, the green and lucent head fades from the screen. Some of the questions this experiment raises are discussed around a long table in a book-lined room during the next sequence of the film. It was shot on the single available day – Labour Day, conveniently for David, falls during September in the United States – in the Air Force Academy's Kimble Library, with the single camera forcing constant delays as new angles demanded new set-ups, involving repetitions, new starts, unwanted and unexpected pauses and a general loss of spontaneity. Two hours of talk produced some ten minutes of film, but those ten minutes were filled with fascinating information and analysis. Dr Robinson, who had flown the Atlantic and more than half the American continent to take part, acted as the simple man who interpreted the jargon of the scientists into language anyone might use. The two professorial Captains, Jumper and Jackson, were joined by Dr Donald Lynn, of the world-famous Jet Propulsion Laboratory, who had flown, also for this one day's filming, from its headquarters in Pasadena, California.

They first discussed the possibility that the Shroud image had been painted by an artist. Capt Jumper, like most other scientists, thought this highly implausible. 'The most likely pigment would have been an organic one ... We know the cloth was exposed to a fire, and from the damage we can tell that it probably went through a very large variation in temperature and this would have been reflected in a change in the colouration of the organic pigment. So I think we can rule that one out, because we don't see that.' Dr Lynn had some relevant results to add to this. They had performed a frequency analysis of the image and the results showed no directionality at all.

'You mean', asked Dr Robinson, playing the plain man, 'something like brushmarks?'

'Yes. If it had been done by a human hand, you'd expect to have preferential direction or directions and not a random orientation as we see in our analysis.'

They then debated the second most common suggestion, that of an exudation from the body causing the image, and dismissed this on two counts. First, as Capt Jumper explains, blood would soak through the cloth, 'but of course we know that the image on the Shroud is a purely surface phenomenon. Secondly, an image produced by pressing a cloth around a body would, when straightened, be too distorted to be very informative or in any way faithful to the original.

'Well', says Dr Robinson, everyone's spokesman, 'you seem to have scotched the two most obvious hypotheses, so what are we left with?' This time, it is Capt Jackson who replies. His colour analysis has shown that the 'variation of the body image and the burn marks fall along the same colour curve', and when Dr Robinson asks him pointblank whether he is saying that both were caused by scorching, he replies that, within the resolution allowed him by his analytical techniques, he 'cannot discriminate between the colour variation of the body image and the burn image.'

He is telling the other three, and us, that the Shroud image is a kind of controlled scorch mark. 'In fact', he says, 'a scorch would answer a few questions for us.' Capt Jumper agrees – for example, the sensitivity to temperature variation, which is one of the main objections to organic pigments having been used, would not apply. It is Dr Lynn, however, who adds the new and still startling idea.

'Also', he tells us, leaning over the table, 'the fact that it's very much of a surface effect would tend to indicate that it's probably a short time-scale phenomenon such as a burst of radiation.'

'What do you mean by a short time?' asks Dr Robinson on cue, to disentangle the jargon.

'Small fractions of a second, as opposed to seconds or minutes, as you'd get with the diffusion process.'

'So you're talking about some momentary burst of energy?'

'That's correct – but not enough energy to destroy the cloth.'

It was during this period of filming that David sensed, for the first time, a deeper involvement in the crew. Most of the men now in front of their camera were neither clergymen nor scholars. They were not even 'mad scientists' wrapped in the elegant obscurities that blur the edges of knowledge. They were hard-headed, comprehensibly intelligent, officers in the Air Force or engaged in the space programme, and using equipment the sophistication of which did not entirely disguise its basic similarity to the machinery the crew technicians were themselves used to. Cameramen, sound-recordists, electricians, they all had a working knowledge of fundamental electronics. They believed it could not deceive them. Now electronics strongly suggests that the Shroud was, if not genuine, then an object of unparalleled strangeness. The demonstration they had filmed moved and involved them more deeply than any words could have done, or half a hundred of Ian Wilson's thought-provoking icons.

In this new mood of awakened interest they flew on to Los Angeles. It was as well that they had become so involved because the work they had done in Colorado Springs had exhausted them. Paul Turtle, on the evening when they had finished shooting there, had fallen asleep in an Italian restaurant, his head in his plate. It was time for a day off. Larry Prinz organised a barbecue in his parents' garden, the crew went sightseeing, springs running low were cautiously rewound for further effort. And, ready for them, Dr Bucklin, newly appointed Chief Pathologist for Texas, had flown in from Austin. The Chief Pathologist of Los Angeles, Dr Neguchi, who might have created difficulties over filming someone no longer on his staff, was the personification of friendliness and offered David all the facilities at his disposal.

For David the mortuary, ever since his first meeting there with Dr Bucklin, had been the only place in which to film his interview. Now he had to select the precise location within the building. In terms of vision and sound the most suitable was the gruesomely named Decomposition Room, to which corpses found weeks and sometimes months after death were brought. Despite constant fumigation, the stench of that place was more than the living could long bear. So they chose the ordinary dissecting room. They were to film on the day after Labour Day weekend, and the mortuary was overflowing. For three days the sad harvest of the dead – those who had been murdered or killed in traffic accidents, in kitchen tragedies and bathroom poisonings, those who had drowned, burned or fallen, the foolhardy, the careless and, saddest of all, the suicidal – for three days the dead had been gathered here, until now the refrigerated drawers and the cold stone tables had all been filled. And still they arrived, this endless, grisly regiment, to await their turn for attention on stretchers in the corridors, lines of the suddenly dead lying in frozen parody of the traffic jams that choked the Los Angeles of the living. To left and right the bodies lay, pale, blue-white, some marked by violence, others at peace, and all in white sheets, careless shrouds flung about them like unimportant copies of the cloth David was there to discuss.

Some of the crew absolutely refused to work in that place in that atmosphere. This was the busiest day of the year in the busiest morgue in the world, and they wanted to be well outside its walls. David did not argue; his essential experts had not flinched and the rest, he felt, were free to make their own decisions. He knew that Dr Bucklin, professional to his finger-tips, would set them as few problems as possible. And indeed they shot the ten minutes his remarks take on the screen in less than two days. Used to giving evidence in court and to lecturing audiences of all kinds, Dr Bucklin had no difficulty in turning to the camera and outlining what he had discovered in the three decades during which he had studied the wounds shown by the Shroud image.

'On the body,' he explains, 'is a variety of injuries. The wounds can best be divided into five categories. The first group concerns injuries which appear on the back. They have obviously been made by some implement with sharp edges. [It is here that Monsignor Ricci demonstrates his Roman whip] ... Present on the back of the image are two areas of abrasion located over the shoulder blades. They were caused by a heavy object resting across the back. The second group of injuries are those which appear on the face and on the head ... On the tip of the nose is a small abrasion, possibly resulting from a fall ... In the forehead and in the scalp is a series of bloodstains ... They were made by sharp pointed objects which had projected below the skin and produced bleeding. Their configuration is such that the implement was like a cap which rested on the head.' [Monsignor Ricci deduces here the crown of thorns, nearest proof of the identity of this man – 'A forger would have included such wounds but would have shown them as all artists did, as a circlet. Instead, the whole head is covered, suggesting a rough clump of thorns – almost certainly what actually happened.']

Dr Bucklin, for his part, continues his catalogue. 'The third group of injuries involves the area of the wrist' – these are the puncture marks, with their divergent streams of blood. It was here that the nails entered during the crucifixion. 'If the left arm is moved laterally to a position where these two divergent streams are vertical as a result of gravity, we have the position of the arm at the time of the flow of blood. An injury to this part of the wrist will invariably damage the medial nerve, whose function is to flex the thumb across the palm. It's interesting to note that there are no thumbs in these images. The next group of injuries are those about the feet ... The last of the injuries is an apparent wound in the side. The markings on this image are so clear and so medically accurate that the pathological facts which they reflect concerning the suffering and death of the man depicted here are, in my opinion, beyond dispute.'

So goodbye the charnel house and goodbye America! The second phase of their overseas filming had been completed. David gave the crew time off; they had open tickets and deserved the break. Those like Bahram who had work already waiting for them in England flew back, but the others scattered through California. David himself spent two days sight-seeing in San Francisco, a gentle city of humps and slopes, of Chinese lampposts and two thousand restaurants, relaxing like a drowsy dowager in a frayed hammock on the geology which will eventually destroy it. Then it was back across the bleak Atlantic, where the rest of the filming still waited to be accomplished.

London was that autumn the venue of a new symposium on the Shroud, a follow-up to the Albuquerque meeting, this time organised by Rev. David Sox. Many of the same experts were present, but one newcomer was Max Frei, brought to England on the production's budget in order to do his film interview against a background of which David could approve. Taking over a bare room in Holland Park Road, the art director, Tony Halton, designed a study for Dr Frei, microscopes prominent and worktable visible, charts and specimens at hand, apparatus satisfyingly mysterious against the walls, which would instantly identify him to any audience as 'scientist'. The interview is enlivened at various points by vast close-ups of pollen spores, taken through an electron microscope and looking like the balefully alien planets of some science-fiction fantasy.

These at first are from plants common in North Europe – the beech, the yew – and Dr Frei can tell us, happily, 'They only confirm what we already know – that the Shroud was exposed to the open air in France and Italy. But then I came across this one.' Expert fingers manipulate the microscope; on the screen we see the relevant spore. '*Linum Mucronatum*', Dr Frei tells us, to our delighted incomprehension. Symbols on a map demonstrate its origin in Asia Minor. Other names follow, other symbols; the camera creeps closer and closer to Turkey. Dr Frei abandons the microscope and looks at us directly, perhaps a little sternly. 'The presence of such a significant number of pollens from plants growing in Turkey leads me to one fundamental conclusion – at some point in its history the Shroud must have been exposed to the air in Southern Turkey or the surroundings of Istanbul.'

We know already what he had to say while being filmed in that spurious Judaea which David had conjured out of the Urfa suburbs. In our minds, his part of the investigation will coalesce into a most convincing testimony. Eight different kinds of pollen known to have existed in the Palestine of Jesus have been found by Dr Frei in dust from the Shroud. Now his steady, unemotional voice puts its seal on his painstaking work: 'The presence of pollen from such plants growing exclusively in the land of the Bible and the surrounding deserts permits only one conclusion – that in some time of its history, the Shroud was exposed to the open air in Palestine.'

How and where exposed? But we know already, we who are watching the film. We have seen it washed and drying, blowing in the hot wind of Biblical Palestine. We, however, can forget what directors of films cannot – that the cinema peddles illusions; when, for example, a man walks whistling up a drive and into a house, the interior we see him enter may be ten thousand miles from the exterior through which, just a few seconds and one cut away, he was happily strolling. Just so with that coarsely grassed semi-desert, complete with goatboy and well, in which our pristine Shroud flew its washday flag. It is set, not in the Middle East, nor even in Asia Minor, but in Kent, on Camber Sands. The goatherd is English, the well plastic, the wind keen and northern, far from the kiln-like *khamsin* we have been imagining. Illusion has trapped us, but for a good purpose and to help the argument of the film. We can hardly blame David for using all the resources at his disposal; but yet, with one corner of our minds, will we remember how our eye has been deceived, and be henceforth the tiniest bit careful?

Bahram with a blue filter, an arc-light precisely placed, goats and sheep hired by the hour – so they filmed the Palestinian waste, while in nearby Arlington Castle they reproduced Savoyard Chambéry and the accidental fire which might so easily have destroyed the Shroud. Nuns fold the unmarked cloth – John Weston's stunning replica – and place it in its casket; smoke rises, and flame. Unfolded, we see its sad disfigurement – in actuality, again John Weston's version. The sequence was much longer and very dramatic when first edited, but David decreed its paring down. No incidental excitements, however well conveyed, could be allowed to hold up the flow of his investigation, the terse didacticism.

Now came the days of studio work at Shepperton. For the first time, a set had to be constructed representing the upper floor of Secondo Pia's house, and Tony Halton built and dressed it with marvellous conviction. Set six feet off the ground to permit the actor to climb stairs up to it, it was by no means cheap to construct, but its detail draws one straight into the life of a nineteenth-century bourgeois with a passion for photography. Halton even had gas piped into the darkroom, in order to lend conviction to the lighting of its red lamp, but in the event gaslight proved too weak for filming and an electric bulb was fitted to do the actual work. The moment remains dramatic, the taper lifted, the hiss of gas pervasive, the light blossoming until suddenly dampened by the red shutter, the whole screen glowing a dull crimson (in the studios red filters slammed over every lamp), while we know that at any moment the photographer will begin to work on those famous plates from which all modern Shroud investigations stem.

And then the significant second when Pia holds up the dripping plate and sees upon it the clarified lineaments of that long-dead man whom he takes without question to be Jesus. He hurries to the window; in the brighter light we view with him that majestic face, properly revealed for the first time in centuries. The music rises and swells towards a mysterious, otherworldly climax ... It was playing when that scene was filmed, a trick common in the days of the silent cinema, when in a corner of the studio the mellifluous music of some industrious quartet would shepherd the actors towards the desired emotion. David must be one of the few directors to have employed it since the triumph of talking pictures. Yet here the device works, perhaps linking the audience subliminally with the actor on the screen, Haydn's *Creation* surrounding him in its glory just as we in the cinema are surrounded as we watch his face, his whole body, responding to that sound. The camera moves closer and for us, as for him, the picture in his hands becomes clearer, while the grandeur of the music makes almost palpable the awe and conviction gathering within him.

At one time David had wanted to dramatise a great deal of the Gospel story, justifying the expenditure by a reference to Monsignor Ricci's theories. These, however, were unlikely now to be fully represented, and he determined to show only those aspects of the Passion which would illuminate the evidence of the Shroud image. The wounds on the back meant that he had to show some the flagellation, bruises demanded a fall, the significance of the flow of blood would be graphically demonstrated. But there would be no rabbis, judges, Roman soldiers, no furious crowds or reluctant proconsuls.

Barry Cranfield's body has the same basic characteristics of the Shroud image. Painstakingly, a make-up artist, working from Monsignor Ricci's descriptions, reproduced the wounds, cuts and abrasions of which the Shroud gives evidence. Then, one by one, the mortal abuses described by the Gospels were enacted and filmed. Only when he saw the rushes and visualised what they would be like when a soundtrack had been added did David realize how powerful these scenes would be in the cinema. Because he hoped that children would see his documentary, he took the painful resolution to reduce their impact, to cut whatever might give offence or cause distress. The spectacular fall, under the weight of the great beam, had to be excised, the flagellation to be much reduced. (In the event, not enough to make the censor happy – violence for amusement in a thriller or police series is acceptable; in a serious film, used for a serious purpose, it excites deep official suspicion.)

For a different reason, David was forced to jettison another planned sequence. He had wanted to show precisely how the abrasions on the shoulders of the man on the Shroud could have been made by the weight of the great cross. He therefore had a transparent Perspex beam made, through which he was able to shoot the actual effects of the pressure. On the screen, however, it demanded so much of an audience's imagination that the very effort intruded into the smooth acceptance of the film's argument. It looked too surrealist, too bizarre, in a document already dealing with one of the world's strangest objects.

The final sequence dealing with the crucifixion shows the position of the man on the Shroud as death approached and overtook him. He had moved while on the cross, rising, then falling, as the evidence of the blood-flow had shown Barbet. Now, as he slumped into the last, long stillness, what was his exact stance? What did the Shroud tell us about the man his mourners saw, hanging above them on the wood? David wanted to show this, yet since the man on that cross had been naked, he could use neither wires nor supports. Again Tony Halton exercised his art-directorial ingenuity. He took a white aluminium frame and to it attached a bicycle saddle, also painted white. He then set up a dazzling white background for the cross and the figure on it. Bahram lit the scene with the greatest care. Barry Cranfield ascended, spread his arms, the lights blazed – and frame and saddle disappeared. Very careful scrutiny will in fact reveal them, but hardly anyone has noticed them during a first viewing of the film.

With these final flourishes of ingenuity, the filming in England came to an end. Only one section remained – that dealing with Turin itself. It was time to make the last international excursion.

The making of films is surrounded by beautiful promises that wilt at the touch of reality like flowers in a frost. It is not usually because people are dishonest that their word is flimsy but rather because at the sight of a film-maker some euphoria takes them over which sweeps aside all caution. Yes, they can provide a flock of geese, thirty Circassian beauties, a 1921 Rolls-Royce ... Trust them!

Don't worry! People who accept these pledges should be warned to make at least provisional arrangements for an alternative source of supply. Thus, with the best will in the world, David's connections in Turin found it impossible to provide as they had promised the draperies with which the cathedral had been decorated on the evening when Secondo Pia took his pictures. Yet that scene had to be included, and draperies had, therefore, to be found.

Tony Hatton, the assistant director Leszek Burzynski and one or two others travelled to Italy, an advance party charged with the task of making all ready for the filming to come. The cathedral to be decorated; Secondo Pia's mobile platform to be reproduced; a horse and carriage to be provided, for Pia's passage from the cathedral to his home; permissions to be exacted from all relevant authorities – these were their principal commissions. They carried out all of them.

The first and perhaps most notable improbability was to obtain permission to stop the traffic of Turin – central Turin – at eight o'clock one evening. There could be no cars in the shot of Pia's carriage rattling towards his darkroom with the precious exposed plates. The intermediaries proved to be two policemen who, diverted from their intention of booking the unit's car for illegal parking, were prepared to help in the matter of clearing the streets if, in return, they might appear in the film. David at once agreed; he needed extra people and had actually been thinking of using an agency.

The police authorities turned out to be equally co-operative, although they too expected a *quid pro quo* – in this case a contribution, to the force's benevolent society, of a sum a little in excess of £100. This seems a comparatively small sum to have paid for having certain central streets in a major city cleared between eight o'clock and midnight. Not that this ended the problems posed by this horse-and-carriage sequence. One of the less foreseeable turned out to be the character of the horse itself. The animal was irresponsible, irritable and wrong-headed, with resentment or indifference dictating its usual attitude to work and those trying to persuade it to do some. The only way its handler knew of curbing the unpredictability of its reactions was by doping it. This, however, posed certain difficulties of its own, since timing decided the success of the operation. Give the horse its dope too late and you were faced with a somnolent beast, unsteady on its feet and happier to lie down between the shafts than to pull the weight of a carriage. Give it the dope too soon, however, and you were confronted with a bad-tempered horse the normal truculence of which had been compounded by a hangover.

As a result, when the shot had finally been lined up with the carriage outside the cathedral waiting for Secondo Pia's excited arrival, the horse nicely balanced between unconsciousness and savagery, it was a major disaster to discover a modern street lamp within range of the lens. Had they been alone, they might simply have torn down this interloper into their nineteenth century; as it was, with the police present, they had to dismantle it completely and with care. Then came the careful topping-up of the horse with its favourite tranquilliser, and suddenly all was ready. Richard Hamer, as Secondo Pia, raced from the church, the horse set off, thankfully in a straight line, the camera whispered as though in gratitude and shooting was under way.

For the shots they were to film inside the Royal Chapel showing Pia taking his photographs, they needed the heavy wooden frame in which the relic had actually been exhibited in 1898. This was kept in the chapel sacristy, and the chapel – though not the Cathedral – falls under the control of the municipal authorities. The formidable *dotoressa* whose departmental responsibility it was, refused for a long time to give permission to use the frame. In the end, Father Rinaldi, who had flown home to his native Turin, agreed to intercede. On hearing his name, the lady focussed her attention on him. Was he, she asked, any relation to a certain Rinaldi whose general sanctity had placed him well on the way to canonisation? With some modesty, Father Rinaldi explained that this saintly man had been his uncle. Abruptly, the *dotoressa* burst into tears and, opening her handbag, showed the surprised priest his uncle's idealised portrait. She prayed to him, she said, at least three times a day. Without any further argument, her objections disappeared. Of course they could use the frame – any venture involving the nephew of the sanctified Rinaldi, and that nephew himself a priest, could not in conscience be opposed by the pious.

With this hurdle cleared, another rose up. Filming inside the chapel was to take place at night, an activity without precedent. To safeguard the Shroud, the municipality, absent royalty's representatives, insisted that armed guards be hired. Reluctantly, David agreed; on the evening when shooting began, two men, bearing revolvers, machine rifles and truncheons (presumably on the belt-and-braces principle) glowered at the crew from the sidelines. Meanwhile a platform had been constructed, a replica of the one Pia had mounted to take his photographs. It was not as rickety a structure as the one he had built; a rigid podium of metal, its modernity was screened by appropriate draperies.

With this wheeled in, the chapel cleared, the necessary lamps in place, the cameras set up – both the historic one of Secondo Pia and the modern one of Bahram Manocheri – and the actors ready, David could at last signal the first shot to begin. And there, on either side of the Shroud, splendid in *carabinieri* flamboyance, stood as guards the two helpful policemen, taking part in the film as they had been promised (and in due course to appear, somewhat flushed with self-importance, in gargantuan close-up). The only note of discord was struck when, in the middle of the night, David wanted to alter the lights around the Shroud. The armed guards, warned by the municipal authorities to let no one near the relic, moved menacingly forward. Furious, David yelled, 'You're fired!', but these were men who knew their duty. Ruefully, David gave way to brute force. 'That's the third time I'd had guns pointed at me during the filming,' he says. 'But it's the only time I was actually paying the chaps who did the pointing!'

They worked without break until at five in the morning when the thin light of a grey dawn came seeping through the windows. They worked late into the next night. During the day between, they left what equipment they could in the chapel. Under a dark drapery stood the John Weston replica of the Shroud, now in the black frame of 1898. Some cleaner carelessly thrust aside the covering cloth. Halfway through the morning, the chapel resounded with sudden cries of surprise, of incipient ecstacy. A busload of German Catholics, on tour in Italy, had seen what they thought was the genuine Shroud. Many had fallen to their knees, others stood transfixed; prayer and admiration ascended. One does not know their reaction when later in the day someone gently told them the truth.

Father Rinaldi appeared before the cameras, explaining to wide-eyed children the nature of the Shroud, just as so many years ago it had been explained to him. Once again, his family had proved to be exceedingly useful; if his saintly uncle had melted the heart of the municipal servant, his brother, a headmaster, had supplied the children. Their moment over, they scampered delightedly away – and suddenly there was only one more shot. One last shot! David stared. Was it possible? A single shot, and everything would be over? The film in its glistening cans and the world contracting to the lights, the mechanical screams and squawks, the endless, merciless repetitions, the split-second timings and frame-by-frame decisions of the cutting room? But yes, one slow, lingering pan across the Turin rooftops, the light rain-washed and grey, Bahram once again exercising his skill to surmount the conditions, and there it was. *The Silent Witness*, three years before a pile of flimsy paper in David's office, was celluloid, was voices and moving pictures, was argument and drama, raw material for an editor; was finally, unanswerably, irreversably, in being.

'OK,' David said. 'Let's wrap it up. We're going home!'

EPILOGUE

First, of course, was the sense of achievement. There were the years of hope, of excitement and despair, the apparently endless months of discussion and setbacks, the promises broken and the promises kept, all finally transmitted to his vision as, in a way, he had always expected they would be and, carried across a darkened hall by a fragile beam of light. The screen swirls crimson. Slowly the letters fade into legibility – *The Silent Witness*: the film exists, it unrolls in the clattering projection room, it moves on the screen before us ... then, first, For David, and most keenly, the sense of achievement.

But as time had passed he had changed fundamentally. The Shroud had been so firmly the centre of his life and the focus of all his concentration that something of what it meant, or might mean, had penetrated. The factual existence of that mysterious cloth and the awe-inspiring origin of its image, not one whit discredited by the scientific examinations that it had undergone, seemed to him more and more miraculous. He might have become unconcerned about it, blasé, indifferent. In actuality, the reverse was true. It seemed to him stranger and more wonderful the longer his association with it lasted.

The merely miraculous, of course, need be no more than a sort of quasi-religious peepshow. It overwhelms us by displaying a power we conceive to be divine. The natural order of things in which we believe is unaccountably altered so that, not knowing what to think, we plump for God as the likeliest cause. This makes God, therefore, a kind of transcendental conjurer who justifies his existeence by his tricks. If the tricks are good enough, we pay our entrance money, in sacrifice, obedience, tithes or worship.

The Shroud, if miraculous at all, is not miraculous in

this sense. Not for nothing has it been termed the Fifth Gospel. The tale it has to tell is one of suffering, the story of torture and death which is the last act in the central drama of the New Testament. But if its testimony about that is to be believed – and David had more and more come to accept its witness – then how can one reject the stages by which Jesus came to that last act? The Passion was the logical consequence of Jesus's entire mission, the unavoidable outcome of his life. The crucifixion attested to the genuineness of the ministry – and the Shroud attests to the genuineness of the crucifixion. They are all one.

For David, therefore, brought by his investigation to an inner, personal certainty that the Shroud was indeed the winding-sheet laid over Jesus after the agony, only one next step was possible. Yet even as he realised this, he realised at the same time that it was a step he had already taken. It was not at some moment in the future that he was going to take up his own revived Christianity – he had already taken it up, perhaps months before and almost without noticing it. Imperceptibly, he had become a Christian once again.

There were, he recognised, also factors other than the Shroud – powerful though that had been – which had influenced him. There was, for example, the solid, undermonstrative religious conviction which underlay the actions and opinions of so many of the people whom he had come to respect as he moved through the story of the Shroud. There were the warmth and benevolence, the simple, unaffected goodness of men like Father Rinaldi. There was the reconciliation between science and the Christian faith, diminishing neither and enhancing both, which men like Eric Jumper and John Jackson had been able to achieve. There was the memory he carried, hardly realising how much he valued it, of the undemonstrative beliefs of the people of Albuquerque. Seeing the priests among them, they had called out happily, 'Good to see you, Father', and 'God be with you', and 'God walks with all of us – hallelujah!' just as people must have done in

England in more open and straightforward days. Looking back, he could see that each of these was like a flag pinned in a map that marked his progress.

He had begun work on the film in the belief that if an agnostic, a virtual unbeliever, like himself found the story so intriguing, others would be equally fascinated. He had never calculated that his close contact with its extraordinary subject-matter would so radically alter the way he thought and felt. It was while an agnostic that he had laid down for himself his first principle as the film's producer – that the investigation should be cool, uncommitted, neutral, never running ahead of the evidence and never sermonising or displaying the slightest missionary fervour. It is clear from the result that he was able to maintain this detachment to the end, keeping separate the progress of the documentary from the development of his own renewed faith.

The Silent Witness had wrought a profound alteration in him, at many levels and in many ways. That his career would perhaps be changed by his bringing the film to a successful conclusion one might have guessed, or he might have hoped for. That he himself, in his attitude to life and in his fundamental beliefs, would be so changed by it was less predictable. Yet the development took place, the difference exists – and will continue, even if the work that caused it should by some mischance be forgotten. It is this which is, for David, perhaps the most important outcome of all those years of endeavour and, in the end, reward.

One may imagine, then, that first showing. Across the darkness the grainy, bitter-honey voice of Kenneth More speaks the narration. An intent audience watches the quick flicker of the final images, visual reminders of the argument which has just been unfolded for them. The narration moves towards its close.

'An intense burst of radiant energy scorching the cloth in a millisecond of time – was this what caused the image on the Shroud? And perhaps, at one and the same time, the phenomenon Christians call the Resurrection? It's a big question. But in so many ways, in the end the Shroud seems to raise more questions than it actually answers. Is it an accident that it has survived down the centuries, awaiting an age capable of unlocking some of the secrets concealed in its shadowy stains? In the words of one writer, only this much is certain – the Shroud of Turin is either the most awesome and instructive relic of Jesus Christ in existence, or it is one of the most ingenious, most unbelievable products of the human mind and hand on record ...'

How will this audience, how will the world in general, accept the questioning of this film, its controlled examination of so emotional a subject? In the days to come, what the press writes is to give some clue. What one might term the 'committed' publications – the Catholic newspapers – prove to be predictably excited. 'If the Holy Shroud of Turin is a medieval fraud', says *Universe*, 'then it must be regarded as a work of incredible genius. That is the conclusion one drawns from a remarkable documentary on the Shroud, *The Silent Witness* ...' The *Catholic Herald* writes of 'the startling conclusions reached by a high-powered team of historians and scientists', one of whom, Dr Don Lynn, 'completely disproves the theory spread by sceptics that the Holy Shroud was the masterpiece of a Renaissance forger who was coincidentally centuries ahead of its time in its knowledge of anatomy.'

In *The Tablet* David Sox comments, his attitude perhaps predictably friendly, 'a remarkable achievement ... almost as thorough a presentation of the current situation as would seem possible'; despite some minor criticism, 'the total import of the film is objective and convincing. The scientific evidence is so compelling that it is hard to remember the heavy negative voices raised against the Shroud's claims at the beginning of this century ...'

The Sun has already decided to run a centre page article

based on a book by a lecturer in educational technology at Trent Polytechnic. This seeks to revive the recurrent and always enticing story that Jesus did not die on the cross. Now they add to this an article on *The Silent Witness*, a juxtaposition which has the effect of reducing all research on the Shroud, at least at first glance, to the same catchpenny level. But they call the film 'remarkable' and give a swift account of its more important evidence. And they quote David: 'I was an agnostic when I began making the film. But, having seen the evidence and talked to those involved, I now describe myself as a Christian.'

The *Daily Express*, too, calls the film 'remarkable' – 'Now the story of the Shroud and an exciting investigation into its authenticity is being told in *The Silent Witness* ... This historical, scientific detective thriller took £250,000 and two years for director 27-year-old David Rolfe to complete. Is it possible that Jesus Christ has left behind an image of himself? Or is the work of a brilliant forger, more brilliant even than the international scientific experts starring in David Rolfe's film?'

The *Evening News* says the film is 'a popular success', and goes on, 'It's as fascinating as a detective story, beautifully made and well worth an hour of your time'. Its namesake in Manchester ignores the film entirely, choosing instead in its much longer article to concentrate on the evidence presented. The attitude of the piece is that of a Christian sceptic, of someone who knows that a relic like the Shroud, while fascinating, has little directly to do with the well-springs of faith. In the final paragraph, this attitude is made very clear: 'Just as an empty tomb did not convince everyone of the resurrection of Christ in 1st-century Jerusalem, so evidence about an ancient piece of cloth will probably not convince everyone today. What caused the amazing spread of Christianity then, and its continuance today, is a personal experience of the reality and power of Christ in people's lives.' No one could wish to quarrel with that conclusion; David Rolfe least of all. It begs one significant question, however – that relics like the

Shroud can be, as David has found, the means by which a person achieves such personal experience of the divine reality.

The *Guardian* is lukewarm about the film – 'undistinguished' is the word it selects – but as fascinated as the other newspapers by the story it has to tell. It summarises the evidence, which, it tells its readers, 'adduces ... that the shroud is an authentic relic dating from the time of Jesus's death, showing the image of a man who, in Rolfe's words, "was crucified in the way we are told Jesus Christ was".'

The Times is more generous about the film, explaining that it 'puts up a strong case for the shroud's authenticity, but it is not blind to the possibility of fakery and makes the point. Some people may think it does not make it strongly enough. Few will fail to find it riveting.'

The *Daily Telegraph* prophecies that *The Silent Witness* 'is likely to cause a ripple of controversy over scientific treatment of the shroud ...' and when it goes on public show select from among 'the early queuers' a Mr David Anderson who confesses, 'I am hoping that the film will prove that it was the Shroud of Christ himself.' As if to counter this the article includes David Rolfe's own affirmation of neutrality. The film was, he tells the journalist, 'an open-minded report on the Holy Shroud of Turin and not an attempt to prove its authenticity either way.'

But these judgements are still to come. For the moment, Kenneth More is still posing the film's final questions. Is it genuine or is it a forgery, though in both cases worthy of awe? 'It is one or the other. There is no middle ground. Which is right?' The low, powerful voice pauses, then poses the last, crucial problem: 'And ... who is he?' On the screen the long, bearded face appears, in all its sombre and majestic indifference. It hangs there, enigmatically, then slowly fades. Against another and more neutral background, words appear: 'Produced and Directed by David W. Rolfe'.

David stares up at the screen. Already it seems as though that name and those functions have no real connection with him, the person watching in the dark and unconsciously braced for the comments, compliments and criticism shortly to pour over him. He knows, of course, that he is David Rolfe and that the film is his creation. He takes the same full responsibility for that as he has done since the beginning. But in a significant way the tense has changes. The film has been his creation. Now it is finished. For three years it has obsessed him, has been the focus of all his energies, all his talents. But it has released him at last. He is free again, a different David from the man whose achievement the screen is proclaiming. *The Silent Witness* has changed him for ever, altered his beliefs, deepened his confidence, widened his experience. He feels better prepared than before, readier to face whatever possibilities life might offer him. Even as the lights come on and all around him there rises the enthusiastic applause of friends and colleagues, even as he stands up to acknowledge their excitement, he can feel his mind turning away, turning to the years ahead, sifting other projects, testing new directions, sniffing at the winds that have begun to blow again out of his future.

And what of the Shroud?

It lies in its casket in Turin, awaiting the exhibition that will usher in a new phase of research. In September, 1978, a much more refined and extensive series of tests than ever before will begin. It is these that the Albuquerque Conference was convened to discuss; since then, the scientific proposals raised there, and elsewhere, by a variety of experts have been considered by the ecclesiastical authorities. In May, 1978, it was made known what list they had drawn up of experiments they were prepared to countenance.

There will be a new examination by electron microscopes. There will be ultra-violet and infra-red photography. There will be X-ray fluorescence; there will be neutronic scanning of the cloth fibres to determine whether organic substances such as blood can be found. There will be further dust samples taken and further analysis of whatever pollen spores may be among them. There will be various radiographic tests and the most delicate of visual examinations. The reverse of the cloth will, for the first time, come under minute scrutiny. What there will not be is an attempt to date the Shroud by means of the Carbon-14 test.

It is not clear why, with the advances in technique that have made the use of very small samples possible, this test has been rejected. By its means, at least the date of the material from which the Shroud was woven might have been firmly fixed. The expected fifty-year margin of error is not so great that it would invalidate the evidence. Certainly such a test would determine whether the Shroud, or the cloth of which it is made, is of the right age either to have been used at the time of Jesus's death or to have provided the base for an early-Renaissance forgery. David Sox was reported to have called the decision of the Archbishop of Turin 'a devastating blow'. Dr McCrone was preparing in Chicago to test samples of the Shroud, hoping for results not too distorted by the contamination which may have affected the deterioration of the radioactive isotope (it is the steady breakdown of this which provides the basis of measurement). Perhaps the conviction that it was a burst of radiation which caused the image led to the consequent presumption that such radiation would falsify the test. If that was so, it suggests an authoritative acceptance of the paradox that the more genuine the Shroud, the less reliable its Carbon-14 dating.

At the moment, the Shroud, despite nearly a century of intense investigation, retains its mystery. This is due partly to the nature of the questions we must ask and partly to the methods by which we must attempt to answer them. If the questions are, 'When was the Shroud image created? How was it created? Is it of the person we believe it to be?', then we can only approach the answers crabwise, through a series of negatives. We set up possible solutions, we test them and we find them true; they remain no more than possible. When we have eliminated all alternatives, the possibility we are left with will be our hypothetical solution. We are a long way from that position, unsatisfactory though even its lack of certainty may turn out to be.

We know, from Dr Frei's pollen-tests, that the cloth was almost certainly in Palestine and may have been there at the expected time. We know that the image was not painted – the lack of directionality proves that. We are almost as sure it was not created from organic pigments – its lack of reaction to heat, and all the microscopic tests, suggest it. We know it was not created by a direct impression from a body or a statue – the lack of distortion proves that. We know it was not created by staining or seepage – its lack of penetration proves that. For the same reason, Vignon's vapour theory is unlikely, and the discovery of coins over the eyes of the image makes is less likely still: as Eric Jumper has commented, 'It is hard to imagine an organic stain mechanism acting to form not only images of the body but also of inert objects such as coins.' Dr Jumper has also reported on tests that seem to rule out any form of saturation as the image-forming process. Such saturation reaches a peak beyond which it cannot go. High-density areas of this kind would become apparent during attempts to establish the image in three dimensions, for they would show up as flat and featureless. No such areas were discovered. Despite the splendid eccentric guesses of a number of experts, this seems also to rule out most forms of printing – even if one could envisage a fourteenth-century artist engraving the front of a man with perfect anatomical accuracy, though with some fairly arbitrary omissions, on a block nearly six feet long; folowing this with a back view so precise that it carries 125 clear and measurable marks of scourging; and then printing these using an unknown technique that gives him infinite gradations of intensity, in an untraceable pigment, on a piece of material carefully provided with pollen spores from Turkey and the Holy Land.

Spectroscopic examination suggests that the Shroud image is a kind of scorch mark. Such marks can be caused by various forms of radiation, heat being, of course, the most ordinary of these. Jackson and Jumper have performed what Eric Jumper calls 'very simple radiation experiments' and have found that images can be formed in this maner – provided there is a source providing radiation of sufficient intensity swiftness to mark only the surface of a cloth of the correct weight. The elimination of possibilities on the one hand, the proposing of alternative hypothesis on the other – that is the way in which science approaches its kind of truth. Accepting that this is so, one can say that in the matter of the Shroud of Turin, the area within which hypothesis is still possible has narrowed considerably during the last ten years. The history of the research is littered with discarded, discredited or extensively modified theories. Perhaps the idea that some microsecond of radiation caused the image, in the form of a precise, yet nebulous, life-sized scorch-mark, will also in time have to be abandoned. Is it, after all, consistent with the red-brown granules that so puzzled the investigators of the Turin Commission? And if it is not, what are they and what will they eventually reveal? Nevertheless, the radiation theory stands at the moment as the one best able to explain the phenomenon by which it has been elicited.

Yet, in the elusive way so characteristic of the Shroud, even if it were proved that this was what created the image, the questions that remained would still outweigh the answers that we had. What radiation? How caused? When set off? For what purpose? If it is a radiation burst of infinitessimal duration that caused the image to appear, then this might be one result of the instantaneous dematerialisation of something the size of a man's body. Is this in fact what happened? And if it did, what kind of event would we have described? Are we to say that it was outside the natural order, or should we extend what we believe the natural order to be so that we may include it?

The fact is that even if we knew everything that could be known about the Shroud of Turin, we would still be faced with an enigma. What we thought of its importance would depend upon our prior beliefs. In the last resort, the miraculous is a monstrous irrelevance. It disturbs us, it leads us to question the reality within which we must pass our lives, but it teaches us very little. We are forced to accommodate it in the way we look at the world, but how we look at the world will depend on many other, more significant, factors. Suppose that everything we imagine about the Shroud turns out to be true. Would that really be a major argument for the truth and transcendental relevance of the Christian faith? Or suppose it turned out to be a forgery. Would that affect in the slightest degree the magnificence of Jesus's preaching? It is true that people demand proofs; like Thomas, their faith is worm-ridden with doubt. But the proofs they demand are for beliefs they wish to hold and dare not, or beliefs they do hold and wish to confirm, or beliefs that others hold and which they, too, desire. Before the miracle, there exists the belief. And what propels us toward belief is need, conviction, logic, personal experience, the direct intervention of the divine in our lives. To all that, the merely miraculous is no more than peripheral.

Yet the Shroud of Turin nags at us. It is an anomaly. We probe it as we might an aching tooth. We want to settle it in some niche, to stop it making us so uncomfortable. We want it explained. We have learned not to take the marvellous at face value; when we fly to Mars, the act is not enough – we take a shovel with us in order to test the soil. We want to understand our world, every corner of it and every dimension. To what understanding, the Shroud is a barrier that might, in due course, become a gateway. If we could unlock it, we might discover facts about the universe that will infinitely enlarge the area we inhabit. In the end, we still succeed. We will reduce hypothesis to that irreduceable minimum which can, as it were, bear our intellectual weight. We will be able to take it as true. Further hypotheses will base themselves on it. Perhaps new kinds of vision, new kinds of experiments new kinds of discovery will flow from that. Perhaps we are at the very threshold of a gateway to dimensions not yet dreamed of in our workaday physics.

For the moment, though, only one question obsesses us. Does the Holy Shroud of Turin really bear the image that generation after generation have believed it does? Do we have, in all truth, preserved in its stubborn fragility the true likeness of Christ?

THE SIRIUS MYSTERY

Robert K. G. Temple

How could a primitive African tribe possess a detailed knowledge of astrophysics centuries before the West? How did the Dogon of Mali know that the Dog Star, Sirius, was orbited by a white dwarf neighbour invisible to the naked eye – and only recently discovered? And how did they know *to the decimal* the orbit of this distant star?

In the most exciting new book since CHARIOT OF THE GODS, Robert Temple asserts that the Dogon were taught by god-like visitors from the Dog Star's solar system, and produces evidence that 'one can only regard with awe'. *The Sunday Times*

'A first class mystery and an author full of enthusiasm . . . a fascinating experience.' *Sunday Telegraph*

MYSTERIES OF THE EARTH

Jacques Bergier

What was the point of building a skyscraper in the desert?

Why did the dinosaur suddenly become extinct?

Can the giant drawings on the plateau in Peru only be seen from the air because they were done for people who could fly?

Who could have made sophisticated metal cylinders long before civilized man ever existed?

Jacques Bergier, co-author of the bestselling MORNING OF THE MAGICIANS, has become famous in France through his belief that 'Intelligences' in outer space are watching us and interfering in our affairs. THE MYSTERIES OF THE EARTH is his unique and startling explanation of the phenomena of our universe: a terrifying demonstration that the science fiction of today may be the reality of tomorrow.

THE LIVES OF THE KINGS AND QUEENS OF ENGLAND

Edited by Antonia Fraser

ONE THOUSAND YEARS OF ENGLISH HISTORY.

From William the Conqueror to Elizabeth II stretches the pageant of England's kings and queens and a story of wars and glory, conquest and exploration, usurpation and murder. Eight of our best-known modern historians tell the sage of England's realm.

'Lively . . . bursting with colour . . . demonstrates not only the way to enjoy history but also the way to marshall a mass of facts' *Economist*

'Well-written, terse and readable' *Times Literary Supplement*

'Lively writing . . . a comprehensive history of England in biographical form' *Sunday Telegraph*